AND SO WE BEGIN

THE FOUNDER OF VIOLENCE ANONYMOUS SHARES A DECADE OF EXPERIENCE WORKING THE 12 STEPS OF VA

By James M.

VA's 1st meeting place. December 2004

Christ Lutheran Church - Christ's Workshop in Austin Texas

Do you relate to any of these statements?

If so, you will benefit from this book and the solution presented here.

- I am unhappy in my long-term relationships.
- My work relationships are tense.
- I get the feeling my kids avoid me.
- My relationship with money is not satisfying.
- I would not describe my home life as consistently peaceful.
- I frequently lose or switch jobs.
- I don't understand why people get angry with me when I'm only trying to help.
- I am sometimes shocked by how I treat customer service people.
- My relationships with my children are tense or stressful.
- I suffer from road rage.
- I hear myself say things that I know I will regret later, but I can't stop myself.
- I make jokes at other people's expense.
- I feel surprised when people admit they are afraid of me.
- I blame others.
- I judge others frequently.
- I often believe I am right and others are wrong.
- I assume that others are not as intelligent as I am.
- Drama seems to follow me.
- I often feel frustrated, angry, sad, or lonely.
- I can't keep my opinion to myself.
- I don't have much sensuality in my life.
- My life lacks true and fulfilling romance.

- I struggle with money and abundance.
- I meet my own needs at the expense of others.
- I allow others to meet their needs at my expense.
- I keep score in relationships.
- I call people names.
- My life would be better if others would just…

From the Author

People are under a common misconception that violent behavior is restricted to physical evidence of force. This is only the tip of the iceberg. When you understand drama and conflict, it's easy to see the subtle forms of manipulation that people use on a daily basis to meet their own needs at the expense of others and most often at the expense of those they love. From the mother in the coffee shop shaming her young daughter into moving faster towards the car, to the absent and avoidant father, to the driver who loses their cool on the road, to the person incarcerated for a violent crime, violent behavior affects all of us and creates traumas that go on affecting the way we think and act. This effect is progressive. Left unchecked it will slow us down, and at its worst, it will destroy lives. Imagine a way to identify this societal disease, heal from it, create a happy, safe and prosperous life and change the lives of people you contact on a daily basis. You will find the formula to that way of life in this book.

Table of Contents

Preface

Those of us who walk the path to recovery understand that violence ranges from subtle to extreme. Physical violence may be the easiest to identify, but it is only the shadow of a personal and societal malady. As you read this book, you will comprehend what we, in Violence Anonymous, have come to understand about the destructive power of violent behavior and the solution to overcome it.

Since 1994, James M. has utilized the tools of 12 Step meetings, spiritual practice and therapy to overcome alcoholism, drug addiction, sexual abuse, money issues, codependency, and depression. Despite all of this inner-work, he was still unable to control his conflict-oriented outbursts and abusive behavior, which ultimately kept him small in his career and unhappy in his relationships. After a number of confrontations with police regarding domestic violence charges, he sought help by voluntarily enrolling in an anger management course. The education he received was vital in avoiding prison or seriously hurting someone, but not enough to stop the cycle of abuse in his own behavior or the behavior of those he attracted. He would improve for long stretches of time, only to find himself in the same mess months later. Over time these dramatic events worsened. Realizing that his condition was progressive, he recognized the need for a daily routine and reminder of his condition; a consistent program of recovery from violence. Thus, Violence Anonymous was born out of a desire to lead a happy, productive life and an understanding of the power of the 12 Steps. For months James held a "men's only" meeting in Austin, Texas. Occasionally other men joined, but mostly he was alone. He knew that the 12 Steps had saved his life from the torture of alcoholism and drug addiction, so he kept on, praying for warriors with the courage to face this personal and societal malady.

In August of 2005, while speaking in another 12 Step meeting, he admitted his experience to a group of women. At their request, the meeting was opened to everyone with a desire to recover from violence, and life was breathed into the community of Violence Anonymous. Today, people from all over North America, Europe, the UK, the Middle East, and India dial into conference call phone meetings and share their experience, strength, and hope, on the road to overcoming violent behavior in their own lives, one day at a time.

How to use this book

This book is designed to be a basic text for recovery in Violence Anonymous and a workbook to help those who want to actively work a VA program and recover from an addiction to conflict and drama. Many find it useful to read with a pen or pencil in hand to more easily and readily answer the questions. I personally work through all 12 Steps one Role at a time. Roles on the Drama Triangle will be discussed in Step 1. My first pass through all 12 Steps was as a Persecutor. Next, I worked the 12 Steps as a Victim, then again as a Rescuer. Many of us continue to work the Steps over and over again. We finish with Step 12 and start again at Step 1, focusing on the Role that is most glaring to us at the time. I recommend that you concentrate on the Role that you and your sponsor agree is most obtrusive in your life today. Keep it simple. No need to do them all at once. I hope this book combined with your own actions brings you peace of mind and freedom from violence. Good reading and good luck in your recovery.

Connection with others and with our own souls

Recently I was reminded of a story where a group of people were trapped and knew they were about to die. Most of them chose to use their phones to call loved ones. What did they say? "I love you." What did they do next? Most prayed or acted in a way that connected them with their souls. This reminded me that when we reach the point of desperation or powerlessness, we immediately recognize what is most important to us in life - connection with others and with our own souls. That is exactly what this book will give you, if you work for it.

Foreword / The Beginning of My Story

My name is James M. I am not that different from you. Our stories may contain similar elements. If you are reading this book, you may find yourself aware that conflict and drama are controlling part of your life. You may be feeling the pain of knowing that this malady affects us all, in sometimes not-so-subtle ways, and you may be looking for answers. I claim to have only those I have stumbled upon. I am not a therapist or a PhD in psychology. I'm just a man who found himself at the bottom of a dark hole and found a way out. I may find myself in it again tomorrow, but just for today I am free from the grips of violent behavior. I was not always the Persecutor or the Victim or the Rescuer, but I found myself in those roles repeatedly. Each position resulted in the same anger, fear, frustration, pain and ultimately knowledge, that I was compromising my integrity and forfeiting my dreams.

I have often imagined being a great man. I relate to movies of heroes, who step out of their own pain to help others. I imagine myself as someone who has something to offer the world, some knowledge and courage I can share. But my addiction to violence kept me from that dream. My habitual behavior of desiring power and control over people, situations and things, left me able to see my dream, but unable to experience it. It was like being trapped under a sheet of ice, unable to grasp the life I had envisioned for myself or hold it close and enjoy it. Meanwhile, I was slowly suffocating myself.

If you relate then you may be ready to hear my story as well as what other members of VA have done to heal and change. If you feel that you are ready to do something about it, to make a fundamental change in your life, then read on. If your heart knows that your fear has you imprisoned, then I hope this book will help you. And If you understand what I am saying, but are not ready to take action, I can tell you that I was there too and we all must hit our own bottom in our own time, but please do not lean on this as an excuse for holding onto behaviors that will ultimately destroy what you hold dear in life.

When I speak of violent behavior, I am not only referring to physical violence. I felt the shame of my behavior long before I laid a hand on my wife. That was the alarm bell that woke me up, but certainly there are many more subtle ways to perpetrate violence. These are some of the ways we VAs have experienced violence being carried out.

- Intimidation
- Manipulation and Control
- Entitlement
- Emotional Abuse
- Psychological Abuse
- Physical Abuse
- Sexual Violence or Abuse
- Isolation
- Minimizing, Denying, or Blaming
- Gaslighting
- Using Children
- Economic or Financial Abuse
- Shaming
- Rescuing
- Victim Thinking
- Sexism
- Racism
- Casteism or Classism
- Coercion or Threats
- Spiritual or Religious Violence

Exercise 1

Recovering VAs continue to ask these questions.

Take out a pen and paper. Answer them for yourself.

Intimidation

How often do I use my size, voice, position, money, or anything else to create fear in others, in the interest of getting my way? How do I use looks, actions and gestures to intimidate others? Do I destroy others' property? Do I use my position of power in society to intimidate and threaten others? Do I smash things or slam doors? Do I abuse animals? Have I ever displayed a weapon to scare someone? Do I allow others to intimidate me in any of these ways? How do I use intimidation to get what I want? What do I think I gain from this?

Manipulation and Control

How do I manipulate people to get my needs met? How do I persuade people to meet my needs at the expense of their own? How do I pretend to be someone I'm not so that others will love or accept me? Do I think the solution to my discomfort is for someone else to change? How do I use fear, guilt, shame or intimidation to control the behavior of others?

Entitlement

Do I righteously or selfishly pursue my wants and desires at the expense of others? Do I believe I've earned or was born with this privilege because of my gender, position, race, sex? Have I been affected by a person, group, business or country acting entitled toward the resources of others?

Emotional Abuse

How do I use guilt or shame to get what I want from others? How do I allow others to manipulate me with guilt or shame? Do I use name-calling or judgments? Do I say things that I know will be hurtful to someone else? Do I put others down to build myself up? When hurt, do I try to humiliate others? Do I allow others to treat me in these ways? What do I gain from that?

Psychological Abuse

How do I create mental anguish for people? Do I think they deserve it? Do I deny my behavior? Do I blame others for my experience? Do I insist that others feel bad for "making" me feel a certain way? How do I use my position of authority or power to control people?

Physical Abuse

Do I cause others physical pain? How?

Sexual Violence or Abuse

How do I use sex to have power over others? Am I selfish and self-centered, only thinking about my own pleasure? Have I ever forced someone or been forced to have sex? Have I groped or molested someone? Have I been groped or molested? Have I raped? Have I been raped? Do I manipulate to get sex? Do I withhold sex to remain in control of a relationship? Do I passively allow sex to happen? Is my sexual behavior in line with my needs and feelings?

Isolation

Do I use jealousy to control someone? How do I allow others to do the same to me? Do I allow others to dictate where I go and with whom I speak? Do I limit people's exposure to outside help? How do I use money to keep people dependent on me or me on them? Do I keep to myself to avoid pain or rejection? Do I refuse to ask for help? How do I isolate myself from the support I need?

Minimizing, Denying, and Blaming

How often do I downplay abuse or say it didn't happen? Do I shift the responsibility of my behavior to someone else? Who do I think caused this situation? How do I let others minimize, deny, or blame me for their part in a matter? How am I complicit in allowing abuse to be carried out? What do I gain from doing this?

Gaslighting

Do I deny that I do hurtful things? Do I deny that the hurtful thing happened? Do I refuse to believe that others might suffer from my behavior? Do I accuse others of doing what I'm actually doing?

Using Children

Do I use a child or children to relay negative messages to others? Do I threaten to take away the children or limit visitation? How do I use guilt about the children to control my partner? How was I used as a child? Could I be repeating the same patterns with children in my care?

Economic or Financial Abuse

How often do I hide income or expenses from my family, employer or business partners? Do I sabotage others' work and income? Do I create or involve myself in drama regarding work and money situations? Do I pressure myself or my partner into a lifestyle beyond our means? Do I deprive myself of financial prosperity? Do I prevent others from getting work? Do I strive for monopoly or do I share? How often am I rude to a customer service representative? Does my financial violence reveal itself in deals that take unnecessary advantage of the naïve? How do I let others hold money or power over my head to get what they want? How do I compromise my integrity for money or power? Do I present false information to gain money or power? Do I get what I really want from these behaviors?

Shaming

How do I subject others to disgrace or humiliation? How do I act out on others because I don't know how to own and verbalize my feelings? How do I continue the cycle of shame by repeating or reenacting the abuses I suffered upon others?

Rescuing

Do I agree to things I don't want to do or know are not in my best interest? Do I behave in co-dependent ways? How do I deny who I am and what I need so that I can be accepted and loved by others? Do I care-take others hoping one day they will care for me? Do I believe I must take care of others to have value as a person? Am I often trying to prove my worth? Do I overexert or exhaust myself and then wonder why others won't do their part?

Victim Thinking

How often do I complain? How often do I think others are responsible for my experience? Am I often frustrated, angry, sad, scared, or depressed? Do I judge people? Do I blame people? How often do I believe "I can't do it" or "I can't take care of myself"?

Sexism

How often do I judge, stereotype or discriminate based on sexual orientation, preference or gender? How do I use my sexual orientation as a tool to manipulate or oppress others? Do I get upset when people of a different sexual orientation don't think or act like I do? Do I think I'm superior to others? Am I afraid if I consider others, I won't get my way? How do I allow others to make decisions that impact me or people like me without considering my needs?

Racism

How have I been treated unfairly based on my race or color? What advantages do I have based on my color or race? Do I discriminate based on the color of someone's skin or their ethnicity? Do I think I'm superior to others? Do I feel fear, anger, or pity when I think about people of races different from mine? How am I prejudiced against people of other color or race? Am I naive about someone else's culture and beliefs and then upset when they don't act like I do? Do I make decisions that would affect others without properly considering them? Am I afraid if I consider others I won't get my way? How do I allow others to make decisions that impact me or people like me without considering my needs?

Casteism or Classism

Do I believe that some people are better or more deserving than others? How do I see myself as better or worse than others? Am I aware of the social class system in my culture? How has that class system affected me? Have I had more or less opportunity as a result of the social class or caste system in my culture?

Coercion and Threats

How do I threaten others to get what I want? Do I threaten to abandon or commit suicide? Do I threaten to hurt them or something/someone they love? Do I threaten to take away privileges or enjoyable activities? Do I confuse discipline with punishment? How do I let others threaten me into doing things I don't want to? Do these behaviors really help me to achieve my dreams? Do I attract and engage with people who use coercion and threats?

Spiritual or Religious Violence

How do I use religion or rituals to control others? Do I try to convince others of my religious convictions or judge them for theirs? Do I see my path as the only way to salvation and see others as damned or wrong? Do I often think that God is on my side and against others? Do I use guilt and fear of damnation to coerce children? Have I been coerced, manipulated or sexually abused by someone in a position of religious power? Do I believe that I am righteous in my views and others are not? Do I allow others who think this way to shame or guilt-trip me? What do I really gain from all this?

Can you think of other ways in which violence, in all its subtlety, is carried out? Take a moment to write them down for yourself.

Violence Anonymous Suggested 12 Steps of recovery:

1. We admitted we were powerless over violence, that our lives had become unmanageable.
2. Came to believe that a power greater than ourselves could restore us to sanity.
3. Made a decision to turn our will and our lives over to the care of God as we understood God.
4. Made a searching and fearless moral inventory of ourselves.
5. Admitted to God, to ourselves and to another human being the exact nature of our wrongs.
6. Were entirely ready to have God remove all these defects of character.
7. Humbly asked God to remove our shortcomings.
8. Made a list of all persons we had harmed, and became willing to make amends to them all.

9. Made direct amends to such people wherever possible, except when to do so would injure them or others.

10. Continued to take personal inventory, and when we were wrong promptly admitted it.

11. Sought, through prayer and meditation, to improve our conscious contact with God as we understood God, praying only for knowledge of God's will for us and the power to carry that out.

12. Having had a spiritual awakening as the result of these Steps, we tried to carry this message to others, and to practice these principles in all our affairs.

These have been adopted from the 12 Steps of Alcoholics Anonymous. It is relevant to note that the language here is from 1935. The term God is used to signify a connection with a "Higher Power" and can take on any meaning the reader chooses.

Printed with permission of Alcoholics Anonymous

Step 1

We admitted we were powerless over violence – that our lives had become unmanageable.

In order to admit that we are powerless over violence, we must first come to the shocking reality that we have been defeated. Violence has torn such a hole in the fabric of our lives that we are left desperate and alone. We are now coming to terms with how cut off we are from the connection and love we crave. Our means of creating safety, security and significance have resulted in heartache, loss and misery. Each VA member's path to rock-bottom was different, but we all share the same crushing hopelessness. Despite this common unity, we respond to the concept of powerlessness in different ways.

Some of us were so relieved and grateful to have found VA that we were willing to admit anything to pull up from the tailspin we called life. This violence addict knew they were free falling and, with help, might avoid hitting the ground with a deafening thud. This newcomer had little problem admitting complete defeat and was aware that their life was unmanageable.

Others met the idea of complete defeat with revolt. As survivors of violence, we pride ourselves on our tenacity and strong will to survive, which makes surrender even harder. "Why should I admit that I'm beaten?" cries this VA newcomer. "My battle siren is 'Never surrender'. How can I possibly admit failure?" This newcomer's sponsor might remind them that it was their rebellious mind that landed them here to begin with. Perhaps a couple more years of acting out and expecting different results would bring this newcomer to their knees.

Another type of violence addict cowered in shame at the idea of surrender. This poor soul had been beaten down so many times that their will to get back up was exhausted. They were so entrenched in the "Victim" role that they were unable to trust people. This VA thought, "How can I possibly rely on others? They usually want something from me or will deceive me and hurt me." This newcomer's sponsor will want to remind them that admitting our powerlessness over participating in drama is the cornerstone to recovering our self-esteem and in time trusting ourselves to attract healthy, kind relationships.

Once at rock bottom our chief drive is to avoid further pain. So why does VA suggest that we admit defeat? Haven't we been humiliated enough? The only possible way we can stomach the pain of our failure is to understand just how bankrupt our lives have become. Violence has taken from us all that we hold dear. We are broken. Our attempts to change our behavior on our own have resulted in more conflict and crisis. And if we are truly honest with ourselves, we can see the intensity of our downward spiral has increased over time. Our sponsors speak of a life without violent thought or action, where people cooperate rather than struggle in conflict, where success is not at the expense of another. This vision seems too far off to truly comprehend, but with time and experience, each VA will begin to understand the truth of these statements.

Once we can swallow the bitter pill of defeat we realize that it is the liberating medicine that delivers us from the clutches of destruction. Admission of our personal powerlessness becomes the foundation of our new lives. We had crossed the ruthless desert of violence and found an oasis, just when we could not take another step. Our admission that we are powerless over violence is all we need to begin drinking from the springs that bring us back to normal living and restore our health in new ways. Without this admission, we find no lasting happiness or enduring strength. We understand that, until we completely accept our dependence on violent behavior, we cannot progress. Our sponsors remind us that we must humble ourselves and admit complete defeat. "This is the main taproot from which our whole society has sprung and flowered."

For this stage of our recovery, we were directed to let go of everything we thought about self-confidence. In fact, our old way of finding confidence was no longer of any use to us. Rather, it was our Achilles' heel. We had developed a propensity to use violence in meeting our basic needs. None of us had ever overcome this dependence with our own willpower. Our sponsors pointed out that we have an addiction to violent thinking and our use of conflict to resolve conflict only deepens its hold over us. They go on to point out that many of us are traumatized by the experiences of our past. Our orientation to using conflict to act out these traumas increases the level of damage to ourselves and others. Each time we attempt to resolve an issue by using violence (whether emotional, psychological, or physical) we deepen the wound. Our bodies and minds scream out for freedom from the pain and our solution has been to pile on more trauma, in hope of squelching our inner-voice. Each time making the voice harder and harder to hear until, from the deafening silence, we erupt either internally or externally. Our unconscious minds understand that the truth will not be kept silent, and a volcanic eruption cannot be ignored.

In the early years of VA, only the most desperate could bear the shame of admitting they were powerless over this obsession. Even these people had little understanding of how hopeless they were. Others tried to join VA, but were unable to admit their powerlessness. A small number were able to grab hold of VA in a desperate last attempt to find happiness. This group found liberation from the perilous grip of violence and began building a life of promise and hope. Many early VAs had a good deal of experience recovering from alcoholism, drug addiction, underearning, sex addiction, food addiction and co-dependency in other 12-Step programs, but nonetheless found ourselves baffled by this malady. We had also used many of VA's tools, which you will read about in the upcoming chapters, but still we could not find peace in relation to others. We began to understand VA's first slogan, "It's not the WHAT, it's the WAY." In other words, we had been doing some of the right things, but the way we were doing them was all wrong. We needed a completely new game plan. One that began with admitting we were powerless over violence – that our lives had become unmanageable.

Why do we insist that every VA must hit rock bottom? Few will work this program without realizing that they have no other option. Once we can no longer tolerate the agony, we are ready to try something new. Working the next 11 Steps asks a newcomer to take on new ways of looking at violence that only someone who has hit bottom would be willing to do: to be rigorously honest and learn empathy, to find a belief in a higher power, to admit our faults and amend our past, to practice prayer and meditation, to help others overcome this disease. Only someone who understands these things must be done to live freely will even start. We were driven to VA by extreme circumstances and only by excruciating pain have we opened our minds to the humbling fact that we are addicted to violence. Now we stand ready to do anything necessary to have this ferocious obsession removed from our lives. Luckily for those who are willing to work it, this program works.

Understanding the Drama Triangle

Victim, Persecutor and Rescuer —The states of violence, the roles we play.

"The Victim is not really as helpless as he feels, the Rescuer is not really helping, and the Persecutor does not really have a valid complaint."

- Claude Steiner PhD

In the beginning of VA, we had no knowledge of the Drama Triangle. We started with the understanding that we couldn't act as a Persecutor without believing consciously or unconsciously that we were a Victim to some person, place or thing. We realized that we were making a choice to see ourselves as a victim either from habit or some underlying trauma, and that we were powerless over the compulsion to control at any cost. We knew that when triggered (a term we will explore more deeply in Step 2) we were rendered temporarily insane, and left to our own devices we would continue to repeat violence in a progressive fashion. When a member of VA from Switzerland introduced us to the Drama Triangle and the three roles that we all play, a new breath of hope was drawn for VA. We could suddenly see the whole picture and our "codependent" behavior was finally recognized as a form of violence. The steady and consistent examination of how we play all three roles in different situations has given us hope, understanding and empathy for the suffering violence addict. Comprehending the roles that we play and how we play them has been crucial and fundamental to our recovery from violence.

The Drama Triangle - defined

The Drama Triangle is a psychological and social model of human interaction first described by Stephen Karpman, which has become widely acknowledged in psychology and psychotherapy. The model posits three habitual psychological roles (or role plays), which people often take in a situation:

- The person who is treated as, or accepts the role of, a victim

- The person who pressures, coerces or persecutes the victim, and

- The rescuer, who intervenes out of an ostensible wish to help the situation or the underdog. The rescuer role is one of a mixed or covert motive, not an honest rescuer in an emergency, but one who is most interested in changing the victim to the person that they would have them be.

As the drama plays out, people may suddenly switch roles, or change tactics, and others will often switch unconsciously to match this. For example, the rescuer (someone who believes they are a victim and pretends to be a helper, in order to control a situation), frustrated that the victim will not take their "advice" lashes out as a persecutor. The original victim, afraid of the attack, turns persecutor and retaliates or retreats further as a "helpless victim."

The covert purpose for each 'player' is to meet their unspoken psychological needs in a manner they feel justified, without having to acknowledge the broader dysfunction or harm done in the situation as a whole. As such, each player is acting upon their own unhealthy habits of meeting their own needs, rather than acting in a genuinely healthy, responsible or altruistic manner.

KARPMAN DRAMA TRIANGLE

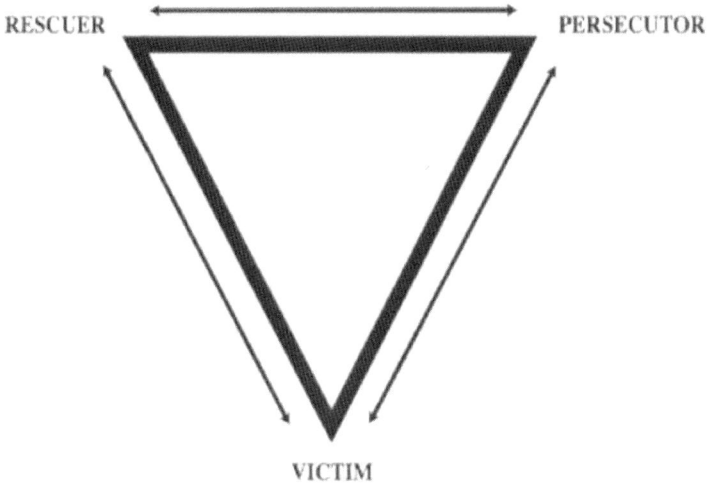

Let's define the three roles further, to fully understand the roles we play and how to identify and correct this behavior in ourselves.

Victim

The Oxford Dictionary tells us that a victim is:

- a person harmed, injured, or killed as a result of a crime, accident, or other event or action.

- a person who is tricked or duped : the victim of a hoax.

- a living creature killed as a religious sacrifice.

In *The Three Faces of Victim,* Lynne Forrest states that:

> *"Whether we know it, or not, most of us react to life as victims. Whenever we refuse to take*

responsibility for ourselves, we unconsciously choose to react as a victim. This inevitably creates feelings of anger, fear, guilt, or inadequacy, and leaves us feeling betrayed, or taken advantage of by others."

Any time I've seen myself as being controlled by outside forces, I have slipped into a Victim mindset. It's easy to do. Here are some examples:

A woman cut me off on the highway because she was on her cell phone. "What an idiot ," I think "doesn't anyone have driver etiquette anymore?" - Victim

Someone doesn't understand what I've tried to explain twice. "This guy's an imbecile ," I think, "How did he get this job?" - Victim

"I've asked him to do it more than once now he's just trying to piss me off." - Victim

"I hate these politicians, why can't one of them just tell the truth?" - Victim

When I think in ways similar to this, I am "on the Drama Triangle" and participating in violent thought. When I act upon any of these thoughts, I am acting out violent behavior. It's my experience that it is impossible to act as a perpetrator or rescuer of violence unless I see myself as a victim. When I am successful at changing my mind and no longer view myself as a victim, I am able to abstain from acting as a perpetrator and rescuer.

Let's go back to the definition. When I convince myself that someone or something outside of me has any power over my state of mind, I have tricked myself into becoming a victim.

Victim - person who is tricked or duped : the victim of a hoax

Maybe as a child you were truly a victim. Perhaps some horrible event shaped your entire life. When I was sexually abused as a 4 year old, I was a real victim, unable to defend myself. An adult who knew better took advantage of me. It took me years of therapy and trauma recovery to get myself to a place where I felt safe again in the world and another few to even consider forgiving. Lucky for me I was willing to go through the pain of remembering such a trauma. Many hide those memories away for a lifetime and stumble through experiences, protecting the wound at all costs. As an adult, I have the responsibility to myself and those I love to acknowledge that I am no longer a victim of anyone or anything. If someone is taking advantage of my naiveté regarding business and charges me more than they should have, do I retaliate at being swindled or do I admit that I could have done more research prior to turning over my money and I could have negotiated a better deal for myself? Perhaps I will report them if that is appropriate and safe, but in order to recover from an addiction to violence, I must abstain from retaliation. If they want to compromise their integrity that's their business, but I do not have that as an option. If I can be quick enough to see that I am responsible for myself, I have a fighting chance to step outside the Victim mindset.

Suppose I begin a conversation with my wife. She needs to be heard about something upsetting to her. I listen for as long as I can, until she begins to repeat herself. At this point I chime in and give some kind of man "fix it" advice (this is an act of rescuing which we will discuss a bit later). She is then upset at not being completely heard (victim) and lashes out at me (persecutor). If I choose to take her attack personally, I have chosen to think of myself as a victim in the situation, and the drama continues. If, however, I am able to remain calm and say something like, "Sorry, I guess you didn't need advice. I heard you say you were frustrated, what do you need now?" I have removed myself from the Drama Triangle and all I have to do is listen for a few more minutes, which for me is a big challenge. She feels great and I don't have an argument on my hands (by the way, this actually just happened as I was writing this chapter).

Take the person who feels anxiety and fear about paying bills and looking over their finances. This VA may make up all kinds of external reasons for their situation. They could blame their boss or ex-boss, the bank, the government, the economy, their father, their mother, or any number of other people, places or things. As long as they see themselves as a victim to their financial state, they keep themselves on the Drama Triangle and render themselves ineffective. The simple act of calculating what they owe has become a melodramatic affair that they put off. They are waiting for a rescuer to come and do it for them, or better yet, fix their situation. "If I just get that big break, I will be fine," they tell themselves. The minute they realize how they are thinking and that they are initiating this thought process, they have liberated themself from the Drama Triangle. They have decided not to buy into the drama of their mind, and suddenly the task has gone from a looming mountain of doom to a simple exercise that they can handle with a little support. If money is not a weakness of yours, I'm sure you can find an example that is.

Exercise 2

Take a moment now and write down the ways you see yourself as a victim.

Rescuer

According to Oxford Languages, a rescuer is "A person who saves someone from a dangerous or difficult situation. A person who prevents something from failing." This definition sounds noble and important and, in its true form, is of great use to society. However, those of us who enter the Drama Triangle as rescuers, rescue for one reason only: to avoid feeling discomfort. Discomfort generated by our own thinking.

Imagine the VA who grows up with a parent who sees themself as a Victim. The parent (Victim) uses shame and guilt to manipulate others into taking care of them. The VA learns that in order to "love" the parent they must take care of the parent's emotional, psychological, and even physical needs. The child (Rescuer) learns to live by the motto, "If I love/take care of you now, you will love/take care of me later." The irony is that the Rescuer mistakes "love" for "control." So what they are actually saying is, "If I control this situation by rescuing you now, you will love me later." Sadly, when dealing with victims, being cared for (loved) later rarely comes, and so the Rescuer is not able to consistently meet their own needs in the relationship. In fact, the Rescuer begins to develop the belief that their needs are unimportant or are only met when they are care-taking others. Thus, the die is cast for future relationships. The blueprint for how the Rescuer relates to the stress and anxiety of meeting or not meeting their own needs is now colored by the guilt and shame of the original wound. Since this phenomenon is progressive, the Rescuer repeats the dynamic over and over, each time getting further from the ability to meet their needs in healthy ways and carrying this behavior into adulthood.

It's very difficult for a person who relies on rescuing to ever see themselves as a victim. They see themselves as stronger, smarter, and more capable than the person they are "helping." As the VA learns to develop their skill for rescuing they may begin to exhibit other controlling behaviors like giving unsolicited advice, "helping to make things better." This may put them in the line of fire for an attack from a victim turned persecutor who resents the input. Rescuers also like to "educate" victims and persecutors about what they are doing and how they can do it better. This is one way a rescuer can maintain the "moral high ground." All of these techniques fall short of helping the rescuer meet their need for security, significance, and contribution to others.

"The belief that we know better than someone else how to resolve their conflict, or are somehow better equipped to do so," Alan Sharland says in *Rescuer Syndrome*, "leads us to intervene or try to 'rescue' them in a way that disempowers them and inhibits their ability to resolve it themselves, which they are actually quite capable of doing. In fact they are the only ones who can."

Here is an example from my past. My father owned a boat when I was a kid. During my pre-teen years, I developed the belief, whether through hints from my father or my own fantasy, that if I cared for the boat as my own, my father would one day allow me to take the boat out myself. I spent summer after summer washing and waxing the boat. I even paid for and installed a new stereo system. I went as far as enlisting help from my friends, so that we could all better enjoy our experience on the boat. Had I been doing that as a way to express my gratitude to my father for taking us to the lake, it all might have been fine. My motive was not to express gratitude, it was to get something in the future: the keys to the boat and the trust of my father. Neither ever came. When I finally asked for the privilege, my father flatly refused without ever acknowledging my contributions. I was stunned and hurt. How could he not see how responsible I had been? How could he be so selfish? Little did I know that I was rescuing in hopes that he would rescue me in turn. Had I clearly stated what I wanted out of the bargain in the beginning and offered my services as a way to show my gratitude, I might have saved myself all that work for nothing.

I carried resentment toward my father for 20 years about that experience. It's true, he did take advantage of me by letting me do all that work for nothing in return, and since he was the adult in the situation he can't get off scot-free as an innocent bystander, but if I'm honest with myself, I must embrace the fact that I was manipulating him into meeting my needs rather than just coming out and asking for him to help me meet them. I could have struck a deal with him that I would do the work in return for an opportunity to use his boat. I could have waited to do the work until he agreed. I didn't. I proceeded ahead without his agreement, hoping one day he would see the light and rescue me as I had rescued him.

As an adult, before VA recovery, I would allow myself to recall that experience and remind myself that I was a victim of my father's selfishness, etc. Sometimes I would even tell him off in my mind. In VA I learned that telling someone off in my mind or "educating someone with my thoughts" is also rescuing. After years of recovery and working through the traumas of failing to meet my own needs by rescuing, today I can choose to see the entire experience in my memory and remain neutral. When I think about that experience, I may feel sad or frustrated, but I no longer see myself as a victim to the situation, in the present moment, and can quickly change my state of mind by thinking more empowering thoughts.

The following are some reflections about rescuing behavior that founding VAs have expressed:

- Offering unsolicited advice is rescuing.

- Rescuing is a violent need to control.

- A rescuer is a victim playing the hero.

- A rescuer pretends to be helpful, when they are really only looking out for themselves.

- Educating someone who is not asking to be educated is rescuing.

- Arguing with someone in your mind is rescuing behavior.

- A rescuer will skirt success so that others won't feel jealous or abandoned.

- A rescuer will seduce people to believe they are someone they are not, in order to get what they think they want.

- Someone who meets the needs of others at the expense of their own is a rescuer.

- The rescuer is desperate to feel important.

- "Since I can't be important to you any other way, I'll at least make myself important to you this way."

- Rescuing is the act of attempting to meet one's needs by assuming the needs of someone else and acting upon that assumption.

- "My mother was so obsessed with her problems and her state of victimhood that I was not important. So I made myself important by trying to solve her problems."

- "Rescuing is compulsively doing something that I don't want to do in order to make someone give me something they can't give, then feeling like a victim as a result."

- Rescuer – "I'll give you your fantasy and you give me mine." When that fails, the rescuer might turn to the persecutor role to get those needs met.

- "I was afraid that if I had needs I would lose the relationship."

Exercise 3

Take a moment now and write down the ways you see yourself as a rescuer.

Persecutor, Perpetrator, Abuser

"Persecutors or Perpetrators identify themselves primarily as victims. They are usually in complete denial about their blaming tactics. When it is pointed out to them, they argue that attack is warranted and necessary for self-protection."

- Lynne Forrest, *The Three Faces of Victim*

Persecute: Subject (someone) to hostility and ill treatment. Harass or annoy (someone).

– Oxford Dictionary.

As Persecutors we act out physical, psychological and emotional violence. It's easy to understand how a physical assault is violent behavior, but what about abusive words, mind games, lies, and other manipulations? We in VA have learned, sometimes the hard way, that these types of psychological "power-over" tactics are also violent. Only when I have convinced myself that I am a victim can I act as a persecutor or perpetrator. It is that simple. Even though we may not yet be conscious of this phenomenon, it is happening every time we jump on the Drama Triangle (something we will discuss a little later). We see ourselves as a victim to some person, place, thing or situation and "bang" we attack. How many times have we felt frightened by someone's behavior and justified retaliation? "They hurt me, so they deserved it." Or "They were about to hurt me so I struck first." How many times have we heard someone say something "wrong" and thought of ourselves as "better than them"? "They don't know what they are talking about, they are a _____." Once I stopped using violent physical behavior, I had no choice but to notice my violent thoughts. When we act out violence our thoughts create emotions. If we do not have the discipline to notice and sit with these emotions, they turn into reactions, often before we are aware of the existence of the original thought. Thoughts lead to emotions. Emotions lead to actions. Actions lead to habits. Habits lead to character.

Exercise 4

Take a moment now and write down the ways you may persecute yourself and others.

Once I have humbled myself and admitted that I have lost control of my habits and actions, that my character has become that of a person who uses power and control to get what they want (safety, security, significance, love, attention, assurance, etc.), then I have a chance to change all the way down to my thoughts: which influence my emotions, actions, habits, and character. In my case, it took the prospect of losing my wife and the State of Texas telling me that my behavior was illegal, for me to remove my blinders and admit that I was behaving violently. It's a tough thing to admit to one's self.

If I admitted that my behavior hurt those around me, I would have to admit that the ways I learned to get what I want were counterproductive, and that those who taught me were ignorant. So, I admitted I had no idea how to successfully function in this world or to achieve my dreams. I admitted that I was beaten by a foe far stronger than me. That violence had taken from me all that I held dear. I was willing to do anything to change from a life of unconsciously seeing myself as a victim. But how do we accomplish this? With daily practice, we VAs continue to discover the answer. If you want the answers that we have found, continue reading and ready yourself for the work ahead. Our first goal is to become aware of our thinking. That may not be easy, since most of us are unconscious of our thoughts. However painful it may be, we find looking back across the landscape of our violent history to be a good starting point. Step 1 directs us to record our story regarding violence.

My story continued...

Parts of my story may be similar to yours or someone you know. To many of you, my experience is too terrible to imagine. To others, it may pale in comparison to the violence you've experienced. The depth of a person's violent scars are less important than their willingness to admit that violence has them in a headlock from which they are unable to escape.

My family of origin was violent. My mother was prone to fits of rage. She would trigger and punish us for the hell she found herself in. She molested and raped my brother and I repeatedly and has never been able to bring herself to admit it. I cannot remember a time when I was disciplined in a thoughtful and conscious way. My lessons came with the fury of a hurricane. My father was absent for most of my childhood and seemed mainly uninterested in anyone but himself when he returned home. He would bring gifts from airports, but ignored our pleas for protection. I remember one time, at age 3 or 4, telling him that "Mommy was hurting my pee pee." He seemed to pretend he didn't hear me, or for all I know he couldn't comprehend what that meant.

My older brother was at least twice my size and learned that violence could get him what he wanted. He, like my mother, would beat me with fists and open hands. He would often pin me to the ground and torture me until I would pronounce how great he was or berate myself to his liking. Neither my mother nor my brother would beat my face. This prevented anyone in my community from seeing physical traces of abuse.

I did run away a few times for short stints, from age 6 to 9 to escape the madness, but found the violence on the streets more traumatizing and returned home, where at least I had a warm bed and food at meal time.

To deal with my fear of being the victim of other people's actions, I developed an attack stance. When threatened, I would take the offensive and look for ways to annihilate my opponent. Because I'm small and smart, this usually came in fast and sharp language. I also have a powerful voice, which I used to my advantage.

As a child, I learned the tantrum. This I carried into adulthood. What started as banging my high chair, progressed to smashing phones, ripping precious sweaters, kicking holes in walls, spitting, and even grabbing my wife in anger. I feel ashamed and embarrassed writing it now, but I felt totally justified in my actions back then. This may sound like insanity. That's because it is. When we are triggered, our thoughts, emotions, and actions become irrational. The trauma of my past had festered into unhealed wounds deep in my psyche that made it easy for me to relive my state of victimhood and trigger onto the Drama

Triangle. Once on the triangle it became easy to justify protecting myself as a persecutor.

I have followed people in traffic just to tell them how terrible their driving was. I have beaten men for standing their ground in the face of my insanity. I broke my hand on one man and spent an evening screaming in pain while a surgeon pinned me back together. The screaming was due to the fact that I didn't trust the doctor to put me under anesthesia, so he and his assistants had to endure my cries while they drilled pins into my shattered bones.

This insanity resulted in job loss, people quietly ducking out of my life, and in the end, the public embarrassment of having the sheriff press charges against me for "man-handling" (probably better described as "unable to act like a man" handling) my wife while she was pregnant, then exhausting my savings on lawyer fees to keep myself out of prison.

This was not the first time I had been at a crisis point because of my violent behavior. Previously, I voluntarily enrolled in an anger management course and attended treatment for behavioral issues. Time would pass and I would get to feeling better, patch it up with my wife, get a new job and forget that I had a problem. Until the next time. And there was always a next time. This disease of violence was always waiting dormant until the next highly stressful moment. Sometimes it took a year, sometimes six months, but it always came back with increasing force and a growing will to destroy. First a nudge, then a push, then a punch. The progression was in full swing with me and I was powerless to stop it. Each time I awoke from the haze thinking, "How did I step in that trap again?!" Then days to recover from the shame of what I had done. This is the seduction of our disease, cunning, baffling and powerful.

As a rescuer, my story is much more subtle and difficult to describe. I learned early in life that, if I could change someone's behavior before they became a threat to me, I could create some sense of safety for myself. I would spend a good deal of time trying to guess what people's needs were in hopes that, if they were happy, I would have a chance for happiness too. What I didn't realize was that I was dealing with victims who were rarely satisfied, and so they never got around to asking what I needed.

Simultaneously, I learned to deny my needs for fear that, if I rocked the boat, I would provoke a violent outburst. Since my family of origin was not versed in the art of Nonviolent Communication, one of our tools in VA, I became accustomed to hearing shaming and guilt-provoking comments. These are behaviors that I can now easily identify as the weapons of a victim to cajole someone into rescuing them emotionally, but during my formative years, I was defenseless against these attacks. To avoid the pain of the disapproval, guilt, and shame I learned to emotionally rescue those in my family, school, and community. This behavior grew and developed into repeatedly denying my needs, and ultimately settling with less in life. I confused the love that I had for people with "care-taking." I honestly believed that sacrificing my needs for the needs of others was helpful, but I learned in VA that such behavior was simply perpetuating life on the Drama Triangle for myself and for those around me. In turn, I began to look for rescuers who would save me from my situation. As I developed physically, I learned to act out the persecutor role when my shaming and guilting didn't work. And round and round the Drama Triangle I went.

So now, as a First Step, I let go and admit that I am powerless and my life has become unmanageable. I surrender. Despite my best efforts, I have not been able to lick this cunning foe. "Stay down," I would hear from my corner and up again I'd rise thinking, "This time I'm faster and smarter." But I was wrong. Now I give it over to a power greater than the one I've been worshiping. Fear and conflict are no longer my masters.

Exercise 5

Take a moment now and write down 5 more ways you see yourself as a victim, persecutor and/or rescuer.

My recollection of Step 1

I was lucky. I had experiential success with overcoming alcoholism, drug addiction, debting, and sex addiction with the help of AA, NA, DA, SAA, SLAA, and the 12 Steps. I know that they had worked in every aspect of my life that I was willing to change. My experience with the steps had supported me through the biggest challenges of my life, and I had always come out of the darkness of addiction with hope and a new way to look at things. So after two anger management courses, 12 years of therapy and 11 years of 12 Step meetings, why was I so out of control? Why was I pushing away work and money, by losing my cool just at the wrong moment? Why was I shouting at my wife when all she needed was assurance and understanding? Why was I kicking in doors and throwing rocks at her car as she drove away, finally having made the decision not to argue with me any longer? And why was I unable to stop seeing myself as a victim in these situations? I somehow imagined that I was justified in hurting others because they had hurt me. An eye for an eye was my battle cry. But I knew better, and my heart was heavy with shame, for I remembered my pledge, while crying out as a child, that I would never treat others the way I had been treated. I had vowed that the abuse of power over others would stop with me, and now I was so entrenched in it, I could not stop of my own accord. I had lost my dignity and I was close to losing my wife and unborn child.

I knew that the only way I had licked an addiction was with daily vigilance and the 12 Steps.

The stigma of the word. "Violence"

We use the word violence all the time. In movie ratings, the news, TV. The word itself is so common that we, as a society, have become desensitized to it. Just look at video games and listen to popular music. It's easy to turn on a commercial radio station and hear songs with violent language or references to violent acts. Much of society condones putting someone down to build up another. Sadly, this thinking has become normal in the 21st century. Even during the middle of the day, there are only a few TV stations I can have on, with my 3 year old in the room, unless I want him to see a murder or some other traumatizing event flash on the screen in the form of an advertisement. These are designed to trigger us into watching the show they represent. They flash on the screen without any warning, and bam, the viewer is left with a terrible image in their mind. So why, in a world where violence is so readily accepted, is it so shameful for a person to admit they have a habit of violent relationships or violent business? We carry mountains of shame about this and trust me, it takes a very brave person to break free. This is what I found in founding Violence Anonymous.

I played around with different names. Domestic Violence Anonymous was the first incarnation, but it seemed to exclude a large part of the way we act out violence. What about the person who has no family problems, but finds themselves unable to succeed in business due to the way they deal with stress? How about the man who does succeed, but at the expense of others, by stealing or lying to get what he wants? What about the girl who is being shamed and controlled by the rules of organized religion in the name of God? What about the grandmother whose children and grandchildren don't visit, because she is too cantankerous? Is she just to rot away in a lonely end to life, or is there hope for her, too? After bouncing ideas off of a number of friends, we chose Violence Anonymous.

Some said the name was too shocking. Who would come to such a meeting? For those people we began to describe the phenomenon of being "conflict oriented" or "having a propensity for drama." How shameful it must have been for the first Alcoholics to admit complete defeat and to acknowledge to another human being that they were an Alcoholic. The creation of AA was in 1935. Now in 2008, it is considered "trendy" to go to AA and NA meetings. It's a part of popular culture. But not for violent behavior. Here we have a stigma of shame that will take years, perhaps decades, for society to embrace. We find ourselves in a time where only the truly brave at heart will be able to take even the First Step. To admit that I am powerless over violence and that my life has become unmanageable. And that left to my own devices I could end up facing prison or death.

I spent months attending AA meetings and announcing that there was a men's meeting called Violence Anonymous and that those who felt they needed help had a place to go. Most of the time, I would hear people sharing about violence in their lives, but they couldn't see what I could see. They had not reached the bottom. So the response to a men's meeting for violence was usually met with a group round of laughter, like "We know we need it, but we're not quite ready to look under that rock." This was in the company of the men who had faced many demons and come out victorious. These men had faced up to the shame of alcoholism and drug addiction; of lying, stealing, and cheating to get drugs. These men had rejected the darkness and pain of self-hatred and found a way to help others. If they weren't ready, who would walk with me on this lonely path to god knows where? Who was brave enough to come? Please don't misunderstand my point. I'm not saying I'm any tougher or braver than anyone else. I had hit the bottom and knew if I was to survive and achieve my dreams, I had to have a fundamental change in the way I operate. I had felt enough pain over this issue and I wanted more than anything to save my own tail. All I could hope to give anyone else was my experience. I did know that I was willing to go it alone until I could find a community of like-minded people to help me through it. I also understood what the early AAs discovered. The only way to keep this recovery is to help another violence addict.

It wasn't until I was sharing on a phone meeting of Debtors Anonymous, that I was dealing with issues of violence and this was what was keeping me from true financial success, that I was approached by a group of women who wondered if I would help them create a meeting open to everyone. Hence, the first VA phone meeting was born. Women from all over North America would call in once a week and we would share about how the week went, abstaining from violent behavior, and how we use the 12 Steps to continue to abstain one day at a time. A totally anonymous teleconference meeting. It was a place to come together, to shine a light for each other through the long dark road to recovering from violent behavior. Some of us see ourselves as victims, some as persecutors, and some as peacekeepers (rescuers), but we all have one thing in common. We seek more grace in dealing with conflict in ourselves, families, and communities. And we all had to embrace those feelings of shame that accompany such a journey. The good news is, once I began to admit that I have a problem, the shame lifted and has been replaced with a true sense of confidence and a desire to help those who come after me. Talk about a feeling of purpose. Buddhist studies teach to turn poison into medicine. We VAs do it every day, by taking the First Step.

Exercise 6

What's your story? How are you powerless over violence and how is your life unmanageable as a result? Take 10 minutes and write it down.

Step 2

Came to believe that a power greater than ourselves could restore us to sanity.

Immediately upon reading this statement many of us raise our heckles with resistance. Since we have grown into conflict-oriented people, it's not surprising that we should rail against the idea that we must believe in a "power greater than ourselves." The VA newcomer may say, "I have already admitted defeat. Haven't I been disgraced enough? Now I must somehow be controlled by some other power. I came to VA because I want to let go of being controlled by others. Now you want me to be controlled by some power greater than myself? I think not." This newcomer's sponsor may guide them to understand that the "ourselves" referred to in Step 2 is the part of us already being controlled by violence. "We are simply stating that we believe there is a power greater than violence that can restore us to sanity. Surely by coming to VA you have already acknowledged that you are not more powerful than violence. Perhaps you might think of the power of Violence Anonymous itself as something greater. Perhaps whatever power you find in the meetings is good enough to start. All you need is a willingness to consider that there might be some power you have not yet tapped in the pursuit of overcoming this painful malady."

There are many names for whatever higher power may or may not exist. For simplicity we use the word God. Many of us substitute different names. The name is not as important as our willingness to believe in something big enough to lift this obsession. Some newcomers don't believe in God. Others have lost faith that God exists, and still others believe but have no trust that God will help regarding violence. So this brings us to a crucial decision. Do we head back the way we came into the dark waters that nearly drowned us, or remain on the shore with these VAs who claim there is a power greater than violence that can and will restore us to sanity?

Let's examine the newcomer who is resistant to change. They say they won't believe in a higher power. Under their posture of strength, they fear they will lose themselves and all they know about living. Their need for significance is somehow attached to the idea that there is no God." Everything just happens. There is no rhyme or reason, it just is." Somehow they think that by believing this they are superior to most and therefore significant. In order to even consider that a power could lift their addiction to conflict would mean complete annihilation of the universe, as they know it. They can admit that violence has them licked for good, but perhaps they have trauma that limits their creativity. To this person a sponsor says, "First of all, the Steps of VA are only suggestions, they are not required. Second, to abstain from conflict and remain free of drama you don't have to swallow the entirety of Step 2 all at once. In fact it's rare that anyone really does. Take it a little at a time. Work through some of your trauma and fear as you go and a lot of this resistance will dissolve as you begin to trust both yourself and VA's simple program. For now just try my third suggestion: keep an open mind. My concept of a higher power in Step 2 was simply the word 'Love'. I wrote it on a card and carried it in my wallet. When I needed some peace of mind throughout the day, I pulled it out and just looked at the word written in crayon. That was my start."

This newcomer is not alone. Many of us felt this way upon entering VA. Gradually, we stopped arguing and Step 2 became part of the fabric of our new lives. We stuck around and, one-day-at-a-time, began to have more productive experiences with less and less drama and more and more happiness. This did not happen all at once. Like this sponsor's approach to coming to believe, it takes time and a desire to change. Their sponsor continues: "Some newcomers choose the power of the VA meetings as their new higher power. Others choose religions from different cultures. I know of one man in recovery who chose a chair as his higher power. For him this was better than worshiping his addiction, and it worked. He remained in recovery and got better. The point is that the path is wide and there is no need for us to exclude ourselves from Step 2 simply because our minds tell us it must be one way or the other. It's enough at this stage to have an open mind."

Some of us once had faith and lost it. These VAs sometimes find it even harder than the atheist or agnostic. At least the atheist and agnostic have a belief. The atheist believes that there is no proof of God, the agnostic that there is proof of no God, but the VA who once had faith and has lost it has no position whatsoever. Perhaps this VA was trained in their early life to become a Rescuer. They drift along thinking that both exercising faith in God and living without God brought the same pain, sadness, and loneliness. So what's the point? They are glad that their early religious teachings helped them to have a sense of morality, honesty and tolerance, and are saddened by the fact that their dealings with less scrupulous people left them feeling victimized and shamed. They may have been misled to confuse "helping" with "rescuing" which led them onto the Drama Triangle time and time again. This phenomenon can be even more intoxicating and damaging when it is attached to their "salvation." Perhaps those who taught them religion believed that Rescuing was being a 'good' person and that "good people go to heaven." Now our VA friend carries the belief that Rescuers go to heaven. It's no wonder that when the pain, frustration, and sadness of rescuing became too great to endure, they abandoned the idea of faith at all for a life of no faith. They would gladly reignite their connection to morality, kindness and tolerance, but are afraid. "I've used faith and played by the rules of the good book only to be tricked and manipulated by others. How am I supposed to get ahead in life when others take and take, exhausting my kindness, money and energy? I'd rather have no faith at all than to experience that again," they say. Their path to recovery will be one of separating their past traumas from the purity of their faith. In time they will realize that their concept of God has been limited by painful experiences that have shaped their beliefs about how to exercise faith.

Often we VAs have been coerced and manipulated into behaving "kindly." Victims are experts at guilting and shaming Rescuers into thinking that they should do or say things that are out of alignment with their integrity. When we behave in ways contrary to our integrity, the experience produces trauma in our psyche that when compounded over time leaves us feeling frustrated and unhappy. Once traumatized, we continue to attract similar situations and experiences. We learn in VA, that the repetition of similar uncomfortable experiences is our minds' way of bringing our behavior into our field of awareness. However most of us continue on without noticing the warning flag being waved. We simply think, "This is how life is. It's full of drama and conflict." Since we have no reference to anything different, we remain ignorant of this phenomenon and perpetuate a conflict-oriented mindset. This mindset keeps us triggered and living on the Drama Triangle, which unchecked leads to an addiction to violent behavior.

The Rescuer who has experienced being manipulated by a Victim into behaving "morally" can easily slip into seeing themselves as a Victim, too. When these behaviors are attached to faith and religion, the depth of the wound can be even deeper and more powerful and the rebellion stronger. When it comes to helping this VA with Step 2, their sponsor may want to echo the words of the previous sponsor, "It's enough at this stage to have an open mind."

There is another type of VA, who has come to rely entirely on their wits. We were like this VA, too. By sheer power of the mind, we had been able to outsmart and outflank almost anyone. We thought "The world is full of intellectual mice and I am the cat, toying with the helpless creatures, for fun and folly. I've never had any need for God, why would I have one now?" We blew ourselves up to gigantic proportions, floating above the pack in an egoic hot air balloon, enjoying the view as we looked down at everyone and everything. Sadly, this mindset of judgment and shame brought us to VA. The loneliness and unhappiness that accompanies this type of behavior took us to our knees and forced us to admit not only that we were powerless over violent thought and behavior, but also that we must find some type of humility in order to progress with our recovery. Perhaps, like us, this newcomer was indoctrinated into these behaviors by others who treated them in the same fashion. In youth they were shamed and judged by their elders, teachers, and peers. They may have even vowed never to treat others the way they had been treated, but in the end found themself powerless to stop this type of intellectual cruelty. Or they may have enjoyed the feeling of power that went along with using vicious words and put-downs. Their sponsor might suggest that they begin to acknowledge their feelings and needs rather than their judgments. This might seem a daunting task for this intellectual to begin, but they will soon learn that by focusing on their feelings, and the needs associated with those feelings, they can create a new connection with themself and a doorway to a power beyond their mind. The simple VA Tool of "Sit with the feeling rather than act on it," might serve this VA well in coming to believe in a power greater than their violent behavior. If this basic VA tool can bring them more peace of mind, imagine what a reliance on a higher power can do for this VA. They may say, "I might try this feelings business, but let's not get ahead of ourselves with this God nonsense." Here the sponsor might tell them, "Some scientists claim that we can only see 4% of the universe. The rest is matter that we don't see or touch. Take the wind, for example: we feel its power on our skin, in our hair. We see its effects on rocks and tree tops. It powers the waves that crash onto our beaches. Yet we cannot see the wind. Perhaps you might consider humbling yourself to consider that there is power beyond our comprehension. With time in recovery I learned to disentangle my intelligence from the pain of my trauma. I have been able to combine intellectual, emotional and spiritual intelligence with humility. If I can do it, I believe you can, too."

Religion and the people in it repulse the next type of VA. Some of us who hold this view watched from the outside as religious figures fell into disgrace with scandal. Those who claimed to be closest to God had dishonored themselves with war, racketeering, fraud and sexual abuse of children. In VA we call this behavior Spiritual Violence. Anyone can agree that these behaviors are abhorrent, however we VAs took it a step further. Some of us delighted in the failure of these people and enjoyed thinking ourselves superior. Other VAs experienced these crimes from the inside, as direct victims and/or perpetrators of such Spiritual Violence. We were survivors of cults and sexual abuse from religious people. We suffered the feelings of shame when we awoke to realize we had been swindled and lied to by the pious. These traumas ran very deep and kept us well back from the idea of getting involved with any program that even remotely claimed to deal with God. This VA newcomer might say, "God is what got me into this mess in the first place and I most definitely will never place my trust in anyone remotely associated with God again." Here the VA sponsor might gently reply, "I too have suffered from Spiritual Violence and I will likely never forget the pain and torture that I endured, but I can tell you that I am no longer triggered by it and in time you too can recover and feel neutral about all of your traumas. You have already shown great courage by admitting you are powerless over violence. The next step is to find a power greater than all this pain that you carry." They might go on to say, "I chose the sunset. To me it was something of beauty that had never caused me harm and that was consistently there, every evening, to remind me of the power of the sun and the beauty of the universe. There is no religious text to follow and only I know what it means to me. Maybe you can find something similar. My point is, if you want recovery from violence, to free yourself from the grips of your trauma and this disease, please try to keep an open mind. That's all you need to make a start."

Now let's have a look at the one full of faith, yet still using power and control to meet their needs. This VA is a precarious type, but not rare at all. In fact, most of the founding members of VA fall into this category. Many of us were long-time 12 Steppers from AA, Al-Anon, NA, DA, UA, SA, SAA, SLAA, OA and more. We were people who had overcome some of the toughest addictions known to humankind, and yet we were baffled by the fact that our relationships were broken, our families were fractured and our businesses were either successful at the expense of others, or failing. How could we have worked so hard on our spiritual condition and centered our lives on recovery, yet still have been missing a genuine connection to God and to other human beings? Without a clear understanding of how violence had colored all of our life experience, we were powerless to change it. With a Step 1 admission of powerlessness over violent behavior and a Step 2 coming to believe in a power greater than ourselves, we discovered that we had unconsciously been worshiping violence over a higher power. Regardless of the name we chose for God, we had been putting our desire or habit for conflict before our relationship with Source. It was this addiction to playing the Victim, Rescuer, and Persecutor that kept us from truly connecting with the God of our understanding. When triggered onto the Drama Triangle we were entering into periods of madness. We needed a power greater than drama that could restore us to sanity.

Many VAs will have trouble with the idea of this addiction being called a mental illness. However, upon closer examination we all realize that the time we spend on the Drama Triangle is time insanely spent. We lose perspective of reality and dive into traumas past and present without regard for what is really happening in the moment. We make ourselves out to be Victims and justify playing the role of the Rescuer,

Persecutor, or both. Upon sober examination of the harm we cause while caught up in conflict, whether it be to the psychological condition of those we effect, the emotional wellbeing of our friends, family, children and colleagues, or the physical condition of the property that we recently damaged, we can clearly see that we have no claim when it comes to "soundness of mind." During these periods we have "lost the plot" and "gone off the rails." Our propensity for victim thinking has rendered us temporarily insane.

With Step 2 we can all stand together, atheist, agnostic, former believer and the faithful. Knowing that, with an open mind and a bit of humility, we can find a deeper spiritual connection that can transform our thinking, lift the obsession of violence from us and restore us to sanity.

Exercise 7

Take 10 minutes to write about your view of a higher power.

Putting Step 2 into Action

Understanding powerful feelings that lead us onto the Drama Triangle and Tools of Abstinence.

Anger (an example)

In order to abstain from violent behavior (my addiction to power and control) I had to understand how my emotions dominated certain aspects of my life. Since anger was easy to spot, I began my exploration there. I could admit that my fears generally manifested in anger and frustration, which led to violence. Having grown up in a family of violence, I had used anger as a way to protect myself as a child. Since I was smaller than my parents and older brother, who was double my size, I often found that outbursts of rage would stop them from picking on me and would give me the space that I needed to keep what I thought was my sanity. However, over time this habit became my first response to stressful situations and I found the consequences to this behavior counterproductive. I soon realized this action was driving me further from the love and connection that I needed.

Other early VAs reacted to their strong emotions by isolating themselves and cutting off from those they feared or resented. They would hide by sleeping more than necessary or by putting up walls to prevent healthy communication. Others dealt with strong emotions by Rescuing ("helping" a Persecutor or Victim). This helping was not really helping, but simply "people pleasing" to avoid the pain of an emotionally, psychologically or physically violent interaction. In other words rescuing is codependent behavior that we VAs employ when triggered onto the Drama Triangle by strong emotions.

Let's take a look at the Oxford Dictionary's definition of Anger.

Anger

Noun: a strong feeling of annoyance, displeasure, or hostility : the colonel's anger at his daughter's disobedience.

Verb: fill (someone) with such a feeling; provoke anger in

I find it interesting to note that the origin of the word anger comes from "grief." What I noticed is, if I allowed myself to sit with my anger rather than act on it, what I really felt was grief or sadness. I was using anger to mask a deeper feeling. This led me to wonder what other feelings I was numbing by jumping straight to anger. The list included many feelings, which could be boiled down to shame, guilt, fear, sadness and hurt.

Exercise 8

Take a few moments to write a list of feelings that you experience when on and off the Drama Triangle.

Exercise 9

Open a dictionary and define each feeling to help you understand yourself more completely. Write the definitions here.

The Niagara Falls Metaphor

Niagara Falls, one of the 7 wonders of the world, pours 35,000,000 gallons of water over its shelf per minute. A few miles up the Niagara River, people safely fish from boats in the slowly moving channel. From there, you can't even hear the monstrous wonder. Imagine if you were in one of those boats and your engine failed, or you lost your oars. At first, you would have plenty of time to call for help and get yourself safely to the shore. However, the closer you get to the falls the faster the current flows and the more dangerous your situation becomes. With each closing second the tension and power of the falls increases and the last 100 yards becomes a raging torrent, until you have taken the plunge over the 180 foot falls into a rock-filled gorge.

Managing the stages of strong emotions can be like navigating that river. Get out soon enough and you're fine. Wait too long and you could be facing what I faced: prison or death. I needed to understand and practice these tools everyday on the small stuff, so when the big emotions surfaced, I was prepared.

5 Stages of strong emotions

How do we accelerate onto the Drama Triangle?

Stage 1   Anchors

Stage 2   Triggers

Stage 3   Craving

Stage 4   Compulsion

Stage 5   Consequences

Stage 1: Anchors

An anchor is a conscious or unconscious thought, trauma or memory stored in our minds and/or bodies that will trigger an emotional response. We all have them: a familiar voice, sound, or smell, being touched in a specific way, tasting a particular food. Some anchors lead us to emotions that we would call constructive. Others lead us to negative or destructive emotions. It's important for us to begin to differentiate between those thoughts and emotions that help us heal, and those that keep us spinning on the same unending wheel of violence. We can place anchors in our minds consciously: however, most of our anchors or thoughts that lead to emotional cues, are set there unconsciously by way of past experience. Many negative past experiences are conscious and unconscious traumas that occurred earlier in our lives. What I had to do, and I encourage you to do the same, is to identify cues that led me to these anchored traumas. My thinking, while reliving these traumas, resulted in anger, fear, resentment and other destructive feelings, what we in VA call the "Victim

State" or being "Triggered onto the Drama Triangle." Often these traumas are not visible to us until we trigger. Once we are able to stabilize our thinking, after a trigger, we can admit that we have some trauma work to do. Now we can begin our exploration with the sticky subject. By tracing our feelings back to the thought that generated the feeling, we can begin to rebuild the way we think about past traumas.

Here are some examples to help us get started identifying negative anchors:

1. I feel uneasy in a negotiation situation. Perhaps my needs were not met as a child or youth when I asked for them. Perhaps I have held on to a belief that I am vulnerable or somehow unsafe and need to protect myself. I may not understand how to ask for my needs without getting triggered.

2. I often think people are out to get me. Perhaps I have some trauma around being abused or taken advantage of.

3. My heart races when I feel cornered. Perhaps I have some strong memory of feeling trapped, emotionally, psychologically or physically.

4. I can't hear negative feedback about myself without a strong reaction. Perhaps I have trauma about being verbally abused or picked on.

Exercise 10

Make a list of anchors or emotional cues that send you into a Victim State and trigger you onto the Drama Triangle.

Here are a number of tools that we VAs use to bring our attention back to productive thinking. When my negative anchors are triggered, I do these things to get my attention back to a positive state.

Change Attention

Often, if I catch an old negative re-run playing in my mind early enough, I can just change my attention to a more productive/positive thought, and it's over. For example, I'm driving down the road and someone cuts me off. I can run the old, "_____ -er has no respect for me" tape or I can change my attention to something else and get on with my day. It's really that easy. At first I told myself that I would become one of those "ignorant people who never feels a feeling," but I found that to be far from the case. Instead, I spend much more time in gratitude and less time seeing myself as a victim.

Change Location

An actor friend of mine once told me when he is having trouble in a scene, he takes a walk outside. He said, "If you want to change your mind, change your environment." By changing our environment, leaving the argument, getting away from someone who is being irrational instead of sticking around to defend ourselves, VAs have avoided thousands of violent situations. In the beginning of our recovery, removing oneself from a situation may pose a challenge, especially to those who are accustomed to Rescuing. With practice and support from our fellow VAs, using this tool becomes easy. We now politely excuse ourselves from the conversation and move on with our day. This allows both parties to de-escalate and reconvene the conversation under calmer circumstances.

Create new positive anchors

There are many ways to do this. The way I found most effective is to recall a time when you were feeling unstoppable, totally confident and happy. Stand up and feel it in your body. Really get it going. Then do a physical gesture like clapping your hands in a very specific way while saying "Yea!" for example. Keep yourself in that heightened powerful state and keep anchoring that specific clap and say "Yea!" Continue this for a while placing your new anchor at the peak of that powerful and confidant state until you know that anchor is placed. Throughout the week, when you find yourself in a peak state, re-anchor. Clap and say "Yea!" If you are exercising and feeling strong or reached a goal, re-anchor to deepen its strength. Now when you need to change your state of mind, or "state," you just fire off the clap and the "Yea!" and you have taken yourself from a negative state to a positive one in seconds.

Exercise 11

Take a few minutes, stand on your feet and create a positive anchor. Go ahead, get up and do it. No need to wait, this tool will change your thinking, your emotions, your actions and your life. Practicing this tool is more important than any reason you may have for postponing this exercise. If you can't do it now, please do it as soon as you possibly can.

Stage 2: Triggers

A trigger is our reaction to the thought embedded in a negative anchor. We hear someone say something with a certain tone of voice, we smell something, we see someone acting a certain way, and our unconscious thoughts based on some past trauma or negative anchor create overwhelming emotions. "Bang!" We are triggered right onto the Drama Triangle. Perhaps when we trigger we play the rescuer. Maybe we play the victim. Or, we become aggressive and play the persecutor role. Regardless of our starting gate position we are now on the Drama Triangle and are acting out violence. This process usually happens in seconds. Whether we experience a mild trigger or a strong trigger, we are irrational and will not find peace until we have successfully removed ourselves from the Drama Triangle by somehow changing our state of mind. Once I am negatively triggered I am no longer dealing in the rational world. I have opened the door of historical pain and I am fighting against that old experience, while tricking myself to believe the person or situation I'm currently dealing with is the true culprit. If it's difficult for you to see in yourself, think of a time when someone you know has acted irrationally about something. It was impossible to reason with that person at the time. Even if you did what they asked, they were still unsatisfied and upset. That is how people act when they are negatively triggered. I had to trust my wife and friends to tell me I was triggered. I had to force myself to listen to them and believe them. Only then could I actually recognize how being triggered felt. To me it is like bad acting. I would go into tantrums or big rages that felt totally false. This was exactly what I disliked about soap operas: the fake emotions. Now I could see I was starring in my own bad soap. Eventually I began to be able to watch myself as if this was an echo of myself and not the true me.

Exercise 12

Make a list of the times when you have triggered and the effects of such behavior.

Exercise 13

What thoughts and beliefs, anchored in your mind, were calling out to be noticed?

Here are some tools we VAs use to bring ourselves back from a trigger.

Belly Breathing – (from "fight or flight" to "I'm alright")

This is perhaps the simplest way to slow down one's thoughts. Rather than sending your attention to your head and the very thoughts that keep you enslaved, try putting your focus on your breathing. You must practice this every day to prepare yourself for the moments when your wellbeing depends on its use. Inhale and let your entire belly and lower back expand like a balloon. Fill up with more air than you think you can hold or are accustomed to taking in. Now when you exhale, drive the air out steadily by pushing your navel toward your spine. Again push further than you are accustomed. Your chest should float upward, remaining full as you release the air, so as not to collapse downward. Repeat this for 10-20 breaths. When you feel your heart rate accelerate and your pulse begin to quicken, recognize you are in the path of an emotional storm and are accelerating toward potential violent thoughts. Use this technique to regain your composure and to redirect your brain's response from "fight or flight" to "I'm alright." This allows us to sit with the feeling rather than act on it.

Processing (neutralizing) a Trigger using Reframing – a graduation exercise

Now that you have re-established some form of calm by belly breathing you can try this tool. Reframing was taught to me by a trusted therapist, and it works like this. Suppose I have triggered. My son is not getting himself into the car fast enough and we are late. I find myself feeling more and more stressed, my heart rate begins to accelerate and I have reached the "steam coming out of my ears" point of no return. I know that I have triggered and I am now in the grips of the "Victim State." I see myself as a victim to this situation and I am ready to act out to protect myself (meet my needs). I step away from the car, take some belly breaths and then begin reframing. Now I search for a way that I can take responsibility without blaming myself or any person, place, or thing, for this situation. This takes the power away from the situation, over which I have no control, and gives it back to me.

First I identify, "What is my belief about this emotional state?" I believe my son doesn't respect me and I hate being late.

Now I have something to work with. You may think I'm nuts, but I believe that there is a part of me that I have unconsciously asked to create situations for my evolution. Here is one right before my very eyes, I call upon that part of myself, sometimes it feels masculine or feminine, and sometimes I even hear a name for it. For now, let's call it an

"Inner Voice." I begin graduating that part of me.

The dialogue with myself goes something like this:

Me (Moderator): "Thank you for creating situations where I feel disrespected and the stress of being late. I am very grateful for your service and for doing just what I asked you to do for so many years. You have created situations like this for me most of my life and you have done it with great precision. Today is your graduation day. A day for you to be promoted, if you wish, to a new position. Congratulations!"

Now I let the part of me that has been working so hard at creating triggered situations like this, give a speech. It may say something like this.

Inner Voice: "Well it's true I have worked very hard and at times it has been exhausting, but ultimately I enjoyed it. I couldn't have done it without the help of some people and situations who I want to thank now. Thanks to my son, who helped by participating in this situation and thanks to my father who usually ran late and thanks to my mother who was always uptight about how I got ready for appointments. Thanks to my boss who is frightening if I'm late. I am now ready to release these duties and my new role will be making sure that we are always 10 minutes early for appointments, so that we can enjoy the ride. I will make extra time for the unexpected and allow my son to take his time, too."

Me: Thanks for your service. Is there any assistance you need to succeed in your new job?

This may work for many of you and may not for others. I find it gets me back on the page of feeling empowered and responsible for my part and allows me to celebrate the change in a positive way.

Prayer

Prayer can be a very powerful tool. There are many prayers that can be used to guide us off the Drama Triangle. You may have many you already use. I like this one. It works for me every time I have a mild to medium trigger.

"God, I pray to find in you what I'm looking for in this person, place, thing or situation. I pray that this person, place, thing, or situation find in you what they may be looking for in me."

This frees me from the grips of my violent thinking and puts me back into neutral. Once my thoughts and feelings about the situation are neutral, I can rationally and reasonably respond in a non-violent way.

Perhaps I should mention that when I began to pray, to really, truly, humbly ask for help from a higher power I was 26 and recovering from alcoholism. I prayed to David Bowie. That's right, sounds crazy, but I know people who prayed to a chair or even made an AA meeting their higher power, so why not Bowie? I had completely lost faith in the God that was thrust upon me as a child. Having been a product of Religious or Spiritual violence and having grown up in an environment where my mother used "burning in hell" as a persuasion method to bend me to her will, I rejected religion with the fury of a hurricane. So when I found myself in need of the help and peace of mind that no man could provide, I was humbled to admit that there are forces at work beyond my explanation and that my surrender to that idea was inevitable if I were to survive. This was when I decided I must be sober to remain alive. August of 1994. So, since I had no belief in the hypocrisy and cruelty of spirituality as outlined by my violent past, I had to start anew. Since I was inspired by Bowie and had his poster hanging on my bathroom wall, as ridiculous as it may sound, I would look into his one blue eye and pray for the courage to remain sober for just that day. Later, with the guidance of friends and my sponsor, I learned new prayers and ways to pray. My prayer life has evolved in a way that works for me, but without a start I was destined for the same agony I had found in drugs and drink. So when I was well enough to face my violent behavior and see it as perhaps the cause for all my other addictions, I had some 11 years of practice under my belt.

In my early VA recovery, if I knew I was triggered I would leave the scene and distance myself before prayer had any effect at all to reduce a craving for violence (believing I was a victim to some person, place or thing). The main consideration for my prayer is my willingness to ask for help, a distinct change from the man who insisted he knew how to solve situations using fear and manipulation to gain power and control.

There are thousands of prayers that have been uttered for centuries and I encourage you to find many that resonate with you.

Exercise 14

Write a prayer that you might use when faced with a trigger.

Trauma Therapy – EMDR

There are many forms of successful therapies that help millions of people become happier, healthier, and more productive members of our global society. I use EMDR (Eye Movement Desensitization and Reprocessing) therapy. With EMDR I have learned to neutralize a trauma in less than 5 minutes. I began employing it with a trusted certified EMDR practitioner during one-hour therapy sessions. After years of practice, I am now able to turn a traumatic anchor (that has led me to trigger) into a neutral/empowering experience in minutes. I've been able to excavate most of the traumatic experiences from my past and am now able to use EMDR therapy as a means of creating peak performance that leads to daily successes in my life. Those of you who take this program to heart by working the 12 Steps and using the tools will understand the power of trauma therapy. EMDR has been one of the most powerful tools in my first 10 years of VA recovery and has helped me work the 12 Steps of VA with a clearer understanding of how my own thinking is affected by violence.

By the time you read this book there will likely be new technologies and methods of rapidly rewiring our minds and replacing trauma with neutral and empowering experience. All of these tools are vital to our recovery from violent thinking and acting. They help us to recover from our triggers and shine a light on the darkness of our unconscious thoughts and beliefs that are anchored in our minds. They are a vital part of Step 2: Came to believe that a power greater than ourselves could restore us to sanity.

Here is a list of Techniques that Early VAs employed to process triggers:

- EMDR (Eye Movement Desensitization and Reprocessing)

- EFT (Emotional Freedom Technique) also known as Tapping Technique

- Reframing Exercise

- Cognitive Behavioral Therapy

- The Work by Byron Katie

- Breathwork

- Focusing

- Internal Family Systems Therapy

- HeartMath

- Hypnotherapy

- NLP (Neuro Linguistic Programing)

- T.A.T Method

- And Others

Consider asking an experienced VA to help you process a trigger.

Stage 3: Craving (Your last warning)

Craving

Noun: a powerful desire for something: a *craving* for chocolate.

A craving, in terms of violent behavior, is the body and mind demanding that we use power and control to solve the current situation. That's a tough thing to reason with. How do we feel when someone makes a demand? Do we enjoy giving them what they ask for? I don't know about you, but when someone comes up to me and says, "give me that now!" My first response, depending on their size, is either "go ____ yourself" (persecutor) or "oh no, I'm scared" (victim) which can lead to "Here take it, even though I need it for myself" (rescuer). Either way there is a potential power struggle. Once we hit the craving stage we have ignited the flames of the power struggle, the collision of beliefs and judgment, the playground of right and wrong. These are places, as violence addicts, we loved to play, but now that we are conscious of the damage that is caused, we can no longer afford to even visit. As VAs in recovery, we no longer want to create situations where one person yields to guilt, shame, or threats and the other dominates. Instead, we aspire to cooperative conflict resolution where both parties feel empowered.

My job in recovery is to remove myself from the power struggle as quickly as possible. Winning a power struggle never creates full satisfaction because someone has to lose for someone else to win. This works in competitive sports, but not in relationships. Recognizing that we are experiencing a craving for unproductive behavior is the first phase to changing our actions and thinking. This phase is called awareness. By raising our awareness we can limit and even avoid the craving stage.

Here are some of the entries from the Oxford Dictionary's Thesaurus.

Longing, yearning, desire, want, wish, hankering, hunger, thirst, appetite, greed, lust, ache, urge, itch, jones.

Exercise 15

Write down some cravings you experience.

So what do we VAs do when we've reached Stage 3, craving and want freedom from strong emotional charges, drama and violence? This is the time for drastic measures.

Change Location - Remove ourselves (Step 2 in action)

Like the wise, we must run from a burning building. This tool has saved me many times. By the time I began to really employ it, I was under investigation by the State of Texas for domestic violence against my pregnant wife and I was desperate to change my behavior. To me this was an admission that I was powerless over violence and my life had become unmanageable (Step 1), and that a power greater than violence could restore me to sanity (Step 2).

My brother-in-law served as a commander in the Green Jackets of her majesty's army. I remember him telling me stories of having to lead his men through hedgerows riddled with land mines. His philosophy was that he couldn't ask those men to do anything he wasn't willing to do himself. It was because of this resolve that he was the first man through the potential minefield. I pretended to be him during this stage of my recovery. My wife and I were trying to work things out, but by no means were we out of the woods. Our conversations easily turned into arguments and I needed a Safety Plan to prevent myself from acting out violence. I decided that I would keep a change of clothes and some money in my car at all times, for easy escapes. In addition I told myself, "Even if I'm in my underwear, if my heart rate begins to climb, I'm outta there." I told my wife as best I could at the time that it was about me and not about her and that I would be using "Change Location" as a tool to prevent violence in our home. I kept the image of my brother-in-law always being ready to go into battle even without his boots, in my mind, and likened myself to a warrior fighting for something I truly believed in; the happiness of my family and my own salvation. When an argument would arise, and I would find myself in stage 3, heart racing and anger rising from the pain of being called this or told that, I would say, "I'll be back" so as not to invoke my wife's feelings of abandonment, and off I would go. Many times I thought, " I need to go back in for my phone or my sunglasses," but I would refuse the impulse and drive away. I told myself, "I'm a grown man, I don't need gadgets, I need peace." I did this for months. The further I got from the house the calmer I would feel, until I was back to a rational state. Now I could do the reframing exercise or some trauma work and get my mind back on track.

Stage 4: Compulsion – (over the falls we go)

Compulsion

noun

1 the action or state of forcing or being forced to do something; constraint: the payment was made under *compulsion*.

2 an irresistible urge to behave in a certain way, esp. against one's conscious wishes: he felt a compulsion to babble on about what had happened.

I find this part of the definition enlightening. "Against one's conscious wishes." Of course in most cases we are not consciously choosing to go into a "victim state" and act out violence. But it happens. Why? Because one of our own thoughts just fired off an unconscious trigger. We know that the unconscious mind is the 90% of the iceberg we cannot see, looming under the surface of the water, waiting to sink the Titanic. But how do we know when it has taken over our actions? Ever see someone acting irrationally, shouting and name calling? Here is an obvious example of someone who has triggered into unconscious pain or fear and is acting out. Some triggers are so deep that we jump right past Stage 3 craving and straight into Compulsion. Snap! We are off the rails and heading for a train wreck. How about the guy who flips you off in traffic despite the fact that you are apologizing for not paying attention? Am I that guy? Are you that guy? If so, you have gone into the haze of compulsion and are crashing over the Niagara Falls, heading for the rocks and undercurrent that many do not return from. Ever have that thought, "I know I shouldn't do this, but I don't care, they are going to pay!" or something like that? Welcome to the compulsion for violent behavior. We VAs are experienced with this state of mind.

How about the person who, when triggered by fear, looks for ways to rescue the other person from their irrational anger? "If I could only change the way I am acting or better yet, change the other person's mind about this issue, I will be safe ," they tell themself. This rescuing behavior is an unconscious compulsion practiced over and over in the past. Not only does it exacerbate and escalate the danger of the situation, it puts the rescuer further from their need for safety. We will discuss ways to identify our needs and practice healthy ways for getting them met later in this book. For now, let us all understand that this compulsive behavior is the very problem that keeps us from healthy loving relationships with family, friends, and money. Yes, money. How often have we wrecked some business deal because we couldn't keep our cool? How often have we chosen not to work with someone else we labeled as difficult? I missed many financial opportunities, because of my compulsion for drama. The traumas and beliefs I held deep inside kept me from realizing my full potential. They hypnotized me and held my focus on drama while opportunity after opportunity passed me by. Without a daily reprieve from such behavior we could all miss many more.

An example of the Compulsion for violence regarding money:

My relationship with money, employment and abundance is an example of how I developed a habit of living in a mild trigger when dealing with matters of financial security and abundance. Founded in a series of traumas over the course of years living with my family of origin, I developed the habit of thinking and acting from a state of compulsion regarding financial matters. By re-triggering myself and living in a perpetual "Victim" state of mind, I allowed my violent thinking to keep me small and failed to prosper.

My relationship with violence and money came from my relationship with my family of origin. If you are expecting some overtly violent story, you may be disappointed. There is no murder or criminal activity. My history is much more subtle in its relation to violence. The violence here is emotional. My father's main concern in life was money. From my perspective, his need for money superseded his need for integrity and to support his family, friends and community. Embarrassingly cheap, he would argue and shame us into never asking for it. So my mother did her best to provide for us three children on her music teacher's income. She paid for school lunches, clothes, sports uniforms, and any other expenses that went beyond shelter. Much of which she did at the expense of her own financial needs. Since my parents had no training in how to meet their needs cooperatively, they perpetuated a violent paradigm of communication in most matters, and especially about finances. My father would play the Persecutor role, ranting and raving when asked for support and my mother played the Rescuer, denying her own needs to avoid conflict.

Like many white-collar working class kids, I began employment at age 10, cutting lawns and shoveling snow to create spending money for myself. I resented it. We lived in the biggest house in our small Kansas town and my dad had a boat and always wore jewelry and bought expensive toys and cars for himself. We even had a swimming pool. But my father was unable to express his needs or hear mine, so my requests for things like new shoes for my growing feet, allowance and fair pay for chores generally resulted in him shaming me or making comments designed to make me feel guilty for needing more than food and shelter. He would shout at us for asking for extras, crying, "I just bought you that!" not remembering that he had purchased something similar over a year ago, and "Get a job and pay for it yourself," a valid suggestion when made lovingly rather than full of anger and shame. What I can see now was that he might have been feeling afraid to spend the money and needed some help, but since he himself had been indoctrinated into the world of using violence to meet his needs at the expense of others, he used guilt and shame to protect himself and his need for financial security. I began to take jobs with the attitude of doing as little as possible and expecting more than my share. This was me looking for a Rescue, founded in the grief and trauma of forfeiting my need to feel significant in the eyes of my father. Since he saw no financial opportunity in my musical talents, and I was desperate for my father's approval, I denied my passion for music, took any job that would pay me and lost the connection between money and fulfillment. This was the blueprint for my Rescuing behavior around money and the source of trauma after trauma as I repeated this behavior time and time again. I sacrificed my need for finding work that inspired my passion and fell into pleasing others to meet my need for significance. My resentment toward my father and my grief of being less important than money to him, turned into an entitlement complex and a habit of looking for success by resenting work and feeling ashamed of my need to be valuable to others. The "way" my father attempted to teach me about the merits of work created repulsion to it. This is the effect of violence. After years of recovery I see he may have been trying to communicate his desire for me to be successful in life, by taking responsibility for my own financial needs. Sadly, his violent approach left me feeling unimportant, hurt, and victimized. I carried this mindset into all of my financial endeavors. "I am a victim and I feel ashamed of the way I earn money." This was my unconscious mantra.

This is the effect of emotional trauma. We carry these wounds around thinking that if we can somehow find success in similar situations, we can win over the trauma. Sadly, that is not how it ends up working. Instead, we re-traumatize ourselves and create a progressive cycle that, rather than improve, becomes increasingly worse. We become addicted to the state of compulsion. Unconsciously, we are bound to the original trauma until we can neutralize it and completely change our thinking. Compound these traumas over years and we have an addiction to violent behavior. We VAs recognize that we must find a power greater than violence to restore us to sanity.

As children we have a natural need to be cared for and loved. Somehow, I saw my father's behavior as a personal attack against me, rather than an expression of his own needs. This thinking left only one conclusion. "I'm a victim and I must manipulate others to take care of me (Rescuer) and/or punish those who don't (Persecutor)." From this state of compulsion, I believed I was entitled to be financially cared for, and I squeezed it out of anyone who would play the game. I was a Victim in my own mind and constantly searching for a Rescuer to meet my needs for me. All of this was, of course, unconscious. After University, I took a job in New York working for a corporation. My attitude was that of resentment toward my employer. Like many of the jobs before, this one ended in my quitting prior to being fired. The sad part for me today is that I didn't even know that I was acting out this power and control cycle. It was my way of somehow having power over the person handing out the checks. Like I was somehow outsmarting them into paying for the pain I carried from my relationship with my family of origin. One boss told me she didn't think I even liked my job and I would be happier in another line of employment, which was absolutely true since I wasn't passionate about the work, but I couldn't admit it to myself. I was afraid of having to face my fears around money and the grief I felt about my family's relationship with abundance. With time and recovery via the 12 Steps I have been able to muster the courage to do work that I enjoy. I now have a career that utilizes many of my strongest skills. I love my work and I am able to provide for my family emotionally, spiritually and financially. After years of healing, I no longer worry that my fears will trigger those unconscious compulsions to transfer my parent's shame to my wife and son. As I grow in my recovery from violence and clear out the past traumas around my need for support, safety, security and prosperity, the level of abundance has gradually increased in my life, both with money and the belief of being truly wealthy and grateful for the affluence I experience. I'm able to provide better for my family and to communicate lovingly about money and our needs for the present and the future, one day at a time.

Compulsion

ORIGIN late Middle English : via Old French from late Latin 'to drive, force' (see compel).

Thesaurus for Compulsion

Noun: he is under no compulsion to go: obligation, constraint, coercion, duress, pressure, intimidation. A compulsion to tell the truth: urge, impulse, need, desire, drive; obsession, fixation, addiction; temptation.

Exercise 16

What can I see about my compulsion for triggering onto the Drama Triangle?

Exercise 17

What strong emotions like shame, guilt, fear, sadness, anger, and hurt overwhelm me?

Exercise 18

What are some of the triggers that set off my compulsions for violent behavior (manipulating others to meet my needs)?

Stage 5: Consequences – (What the heck just happened?)

Consequence

Noun: a result or effect of an action or condition: many have been laid off from work as a consequence of the administration's policies.

I'm sure you wouldn't be reading this book if you hadn't already suffered some of the consequences of strong emotions like anger, shame, and guilt that lead us to violence. Perhaps you have done jail time, lost a spouse, hurt a child, lost a job, money, or your self-respect. After a violent interaction, whether from the rescuer, persecutor, or victim role we inevitably feel guilty, ashamed or embarrassed. Somehow we understand that our methods for meeting our needs for comfort, variety, significance, connection, growth or contribution have fallen short of the mark. Not only do we feel that our needs were unmet, if we are honest with ourselves, we'd know that we have failed to help the other person meet their needs as well. These thoughts and feelings, if unresolved, become anchors for future triggers allowing the cycle to begin again. And the wheel goes round and round. But there is a way out of the maddening cycle of abusive behavior. You can learn to stop this cycle or prevent yourself from plunging over the mighty Niagara. I found a way out in these 12 Steps, Violence Anonymous Meetings and the tools of VA.

Education: the antidote to ignorance

I'm sure we can all agree that education is crucial in understanding any subject. Some VAs believe that ignorance is the root source of violent behavior. By lacking a clear understanding of our own needs and how to meet those needs in cooperation with another, don't we lay the foundation for someone who shares our ignorance to continue the cycle of violence? Might a higher level of education regarding our behavior remedy the problem? Recovering VAs will rejoice "Yes, however education alone could not save us from the voracious appetite of power and control. It was daily vigilance, meetings and working VA's 12 Steps that secured our recovery."

Even after quantum leaps in knowledge about my behavior and months of reprieve from its effects on the lives of my family, violence always returned and each time with a greater fury than the last. It was consistent progress through VA meetings and step work that allowed me to convert my years of education into a lasting change and allowed my family and colleagues to feel relaxed and safe in my company.

We VAs who have come before you, understand from experience, that becoming conscious of our thoughts, feelings, actions and behavior begins in the 2nd Step of VA. By admitting our powerlessness over violence in Step 1 and acknowledging that we have failed to overcome this malady, we enter into Step 2 with an open willingness to try something new; to listen to those who have come before us and have found a way out of the pain and shame of violent behavior. Here we embraced the tools listed in this chapter and sought out as many more as we could employ toward the aim of "coming to believe in a power greater than violence." We have found this belief to be imperative and fundamental in recovering and creating true happiness.

For resources that I found helpful see Appendix A. I'm sure you have and will find many more to add to this list.

Exercise 19

Write down the consequences of violent behavior that you have experienced.

Step 3

Made a decision to turn our will and our lives over to the care of God, as we understood God.

Step 1 and 2 encouraged us to reflect on ourselves; to examine our history with violence and to open our minds to new ideas about how to find something more fulfilling in life. Unlike these previous Steps of contemplation, Step 3 and the Steps that follow require action. It is through action that we can begin to change our habitual pattern toward self-will that has kept us separate from our highest good. Faith is necessary for our liberation from violence, but faith alone will not free our hearts and minds. It is possible to believe that a higher power exists without allowing that power to guide and direct us. For the newcomer this may seem difficult, even impossible. They may ask, "How precisely do I turn my will and life over the care of whatever God there might be?" Step 3 becomes our first attempt.

By simply having the willingness to remain free of the Drama Triangle, we begin to experience a shift in our relationship to the world, both visible and hidden from our sight. Once the door of willingness is open, we find we can always open it a little more. Though a sudden trigger may slam the door shut again, simply returning to willingness will re-open our channel to God. We have found that our VA recovery will depend upon our level of willingness to completely open this door.

This may seem too metaphoric for the practical-minded newcomer. They may say, "I don't know about all this door and channel to God business. I'm not sure about any of this hocus pocus." Step 3 is much more practical than it may first seem. Every person who has joined VA with the intention to recover has already begun this Step. We came to meetings broken by our own admission and turned our lives over to the protection and care of Violence Anonymous. Every VA has let go of a level of self-will just to be here. We laid down many of our beliefs about violence and picked up those suggested by the VA program. These are all examples of willingness to change. Any willing newcomer can see that VA is a safe place for the ball of confusion we have become. We are already living examples of turning one's will and life over to a newfound Power.

Some VAs began this path desperate to save a relationship, a career or some situation in life that, because of the VA's behavior, has now ended. Others want to escape incarceration or to shorten a sentence. For these people willingness may come easier. They may find themselves beaten down by their desire for power and control. They may be willing to try anything in order to find relief from the agony of shame and grief. Others simply were not living the life that would truly fulfill them. Their bottom was not as dramatic. For those, this idea of willingness may not come so easily. They may say, "Many facets of my life are working well. Why should I become willing to turn my will and life over to a higher power?" Why would they want to give up the dignity of knowing that the knowledge they have accumulated in some areas has empowered them to great heights? Perhaps great family fortunes have been amassed. Perhaps amazing feats have been accomplished. So how does that VA find the strength to let go of control? Their sponsor might remind them that violence rarely only turns up in one aspect of our lives. Instead it has woven itself into the fabric of our thinking.

Let's have a look at our society today. Is self-sufficiency really paying off? Mankind has progressed to the point where one can log into a device and communicate all over the world. Business can function without ever seeing a client. Information is king and those who have it are selling their business for fortunes to marketers and conglomerates. Buildings rise and fall in faster and more efficient ways. The sun and wind are harnessed for power to accomplish unlimited tasks. Yet our society is becoming increasingly violent and divided. Men and women grapple for control of governments and countries. Each side proclaiming, "I'm right and you are wrong." The masses are gradually allowing themselves to be ensnared by consumerism and the number of people starving continues to rise. Crime is on the rise despite the increase of prisons. We have wars on drugs, terrorism, and crime, yet none are completely effective because of the nature of conflict. How can we blame those who retaliate from having their neighborhoods bombed, their families erased and their sources of income taken? This kind of thing is happening all over the world in the name of progress. Do we really think we are creating peace? These are extreme examples that make it easy to see how power and control strategies do not produce harmony in society. With an individual, these behaviors may not be as easy to identify. We may find it more difficult to see how our dependence on violence has rung the life out of our family and co-workers, and led them to feelings of frustration and fear. We may find ourselves ignorant to the ways that we injure those around us by depending on manipulation, or a co-dependency to those who manipulate. We may not want to see how dependent we have become on seeing ourselves as a victim to the job, the partner, the child, the stranger.

Once we are truly willing to admit that we are already acting out a dependency, it's easy to replace that dependence on violence with a dependence on a higher power, or at the very least the VA meeting or group. An experienced member of the VA group might suggest replacing our dependence on violent interactions with the tools of VA. She might tell the newcomer that, when abstaining from violence, the VA Tools are invaluable. Making a Phone Call to another VA in times of crisis, Changing Location to avoid a potential conflict, Self

Care, Processing Triggers and Nonviolent Communication have all proven successful in not only preventing an experience of discord but creating an experience of happiness. This VA old-timer would be wise to encourage dependence on these Tools as a practical expression of turning our will and our lives over to a higher power.

Exercise 20

List the ways you need to let go of power and control.

Tools of Violence Anonymous

1. **Sponsorship** – Our experience shows that working the 12 Steps of Violence Anonymous is crucial to our recovery and working with a sponsor keeps us focused and grounded in that process. We seek a sponsor who has worked the 12 Steps of VA and who has experience processing triggers. By being willing to sponsor and be sponsored we ensure our personal recovery and the strength of VA as a whole.

2. **Meetings** – We attend VA meetings to share our experience, strength, hope, and honesty with one another and to learn about the many faces of violence in our lives. At meetings we are reminded that there is a solution. By attending meetings, we deepen our recovery and carry the message of VA to those who still suffer.

3. **Literature/Readings** – We use literature to improve our understanding of our relationship to violence. By reading literature we remind ourselves of the solution to violent behavior and increase our awareness of our thoughts about people, places and things that sometimes trigger us into thinking that playing the rescuer, persecutor or victim will help us meet our needs. Many VAs utilize this tool between meetings as a reminder that we can live off the Drama Triangle.

4. **Service** – Service strengthens our recovery and helps ensure our growth in overcoming violence. Service can include attending meetings, chairing a meeting, reading

literature in a meeting, time keeping, sharing, sponsoring, participating in business meetings, and speaking on the phone with other VAs.

5. **Prayer/Meditation** – When we pick up this tool we acknowledge the limits of our own power and perspective, and seek reliance on a spiritual source of strength. To pray and meditate, it is not necessary that we name or define that spiritual source. There are many ways to use this tool. Here are some possibilities: contemplating a starry sky; participating in ceremonies with a religious community; communicating aloud to a benevolent power, in solitude; attuning to our feelings and needs; reading prayers or inspirational words; focusing on the movement of our breath. In prayer and meditation we open ourselves to a state of being where we can transcend our dependence on violence and experience the true power of being connected to source.

6. **Nonviolent Communication** – We use Nonviolent Communication when listening and speaking. This form of communication allows us to identify and express our feelings and needs, and request help in meeting those needs. Using NVC liberates us, as we discover a way to relate to others while remaining free of the Drama Triangle. Practicing NVC creates the possibility of cooperative solutions that meet our needs and the needs of others. Nonviolent Communication deepens connections and cultivates authenticity and well-being in our lives.

7. **Phone Calls** – We call other VAs as a means of giving and receiving support in abstaining from violent

behavior. A consistent daily practice of phone calls makes it easier to reach out for support with challenges and in crisis moments. Isolation and the belief that we can recover alone are symptoms of an addiction to violence. Using the phone is a way to strengthen our recovery by building a strong network of support with other VAs. We are especially careful to respect anonymity when leaving messages.

8. **Awareness** – In VA we see awareness as an intimate understanding of violence in ourselves, others and society. We use this understanding to choose recovery by responding consciously, rather than reacting unconsciously to life situations with helplessness, attack or control. We develop the capacity to discern when others are engaging in violence, allowing us to maintain a state of neutrality. We have found that our awareness grows by attending meetings, reading literature, utilizing VA's tools and working the 12 Steps of VA. With awareness we notice our progress and our experiences of increasing serenity, effectiveness and happiness.

9. **Processing Triggers** – A trigger is our internal reaction to a person, place, thing, situation or thought. Triggers can range from mild to severe. Some triggers are positive, and some are negative. When we are negatively triggered we are casting ourselves as victims. This puts us on the Drama Triangle, making it difficult to think, speak or act without causing harm. In recovery we recognize each trigger as a warning that we are at risk of behaving violently. We heed this warning, halt, and process the trigger before moving on. Processing a trigger is

investigating the trauma that lies beneath the trigger and neutralizing our reaction to it. Our experience shows that processing triggers with support is essential. We don't have to do it alone. Neutralizing traumas with the guidance of a trusted therapist, peer or sponsor helps us become adept at processing triggers ourselves. By processing triggers as they come up, we gradually clear our inner landscape of the traumas that set off our violent behavior.

10. **Fun, Humor and Laughter** – By choosing to value the lighter side of human experience we learn to let go and to enjoy our lives more. We use humor in a way that inspires a feeling of safety and belonging among those involved.

11. **Deep Breathing** – We have found that deep breathing helps us de-escalate from a trigger or a potential trigger. Taking 10-20 deep breaths can settle our minds and allow our bodies to relax. This practice brings us out of the thoughts that keep us on the Drama Triangle and into the present moment.

12. **Choice** – The habit of acknowledging responsibility for how we choose to spend our time and energy becomes insurance against the temptation to see ourselves as victims of circumstance. We maintain a level of participation in activities and commitments that is balanced and sustainable over time, knowing that we also have the choice to adjust our participation level in response to inspiration or special circumstances. As our recovery deepens through working the 12 Steps of VA, we become able to listen to the intuitive feedback our

body gives us about our true needs, and discover a world of choice we never knew existed.

13. **Self-Care** – Our biochemistry affects our judgment and our ability to respond to situations in a neutral way. The list below raises our awareness of ways we can care for our essential physical needs and avoid playing one of the roles on the Drama Triangle. Each individual may have additional ways that they practice self-care.

- Balanced rest.

- Balanced nutrition.

- Balanced exercise.

14. **Experience the feeling (sit with the feeling rather than act on it)** – In VA, as we learn to experience our feelings we discover that they hold the keys to understanding what our true needs really are. Sitting with a feeling means giving ourselves time to connect to the need that's behind it. Then, instead of acting on the feeling, we can take action on meeting the *need* – peacefully. By using this tool we become able to make choices that are truly in alignment with our heart's desire.

15. **Change Attention** – Many of us suffer from chronic "victim thinking." With this tool, we change the habitual thinking patterns that have repeatedly led us onto the Drama Triangle. We also use this tool to neutralize a mild trigger or minimize the impact of a more intense trigger. If we can recognize an impending trigger, we can use this tool to avoid triggering at all. Changing attention to a more positive state may include redirecting our

thoughts; changing the subject of a conversation to a more positive one; focusing on something of beauty; using affirmations; becoming aware of our body and surroundings; focusing on something inspiring rather than upsetting. By cultivating the habit of changing our attention to a more positive state we increase the amount of time we spend in gratitude, joy and peace.

16. **Change Location** – Changing location is a safety mechanism to avoid triggering and/or reduce the intensity of a trigger. Whether we are triggered or dealing with someone else who is triggered, moving to a safe location can reduce the effects of the situation and give us crucial time and space to allow our thinking to return to a neutral state. By changing our location we can put ourselves in a position to pause and work toward a cooperative solution, at a later time, when we can meet our need for connection in a peaceful way.

17. **Safety Plan** – The safety plan tool helps us prepare for the moment-by-moment challenge of remaining free from the Drama Triangle and abstaining from violent thought and behavior. When we create a safety plan we identify *ahead of time* what VA Tools we can use in a potentially triggering situation and what steps we will take, should a trigger (our own or someone else's) catch us by surprise. A plan for physical safety may include a clear intention and willingness to change location if a situation threatens to escalate, keeping spare keys, clothing, and money where we can access them quickly if needed. With a safety plan in place, in the heat of the moment we can grab hold of the VA program...and

each time we do, we feel our feet more solidly on the ground of our new life.

18. **Creativity** – For simplicity, we define creativity as making, doing, thinking or experiencing in an imaginative way. Many consider creativity to be an act of meditation, devotion, or practice. Others find solace in the technical aspects of an activity. Regardless of how one might define it, we find creativity to be helpful in connecting with something deeper or bigger than our current state of mind. Being creative can be a way of processing conscious and unconscious beliefs, patterns, and triggers and can also help us achieve a blissful and fulfilling state of mind. It enhances our connection to ourselves and the outside world while giving us a potential vehicle to meet our needs for Certainty, Variety, Significance, Connection, Growth, and Contribution. Some examples of creative activities are sports, visual arts, cooking, gardening, work, crafts, music, performance, writing, dance, and other fine arts. Making time for creativity can enhance our ability to use other tools of VA, and be a healthy addition to our recovery.

Here is a list of techniques that Early VAs employed to process triggers:

- EMDR (Eye Movement Desensitization and Reprocessing)

- EFT (Emotional Freedom Technique) also known as Tapping Technique

- Reframing Exercise

- Cognitive Behavioral Therapy

- The Work by Byron Katie

- Breathwork

- Focusing

- Internal Family Systems Therapy

- HeartMath

- Hypnotherapy

- NLP (Neuro Linguistic Programing)

- T.A.T Method

Recognizing gravity as a natural law has freed up scientists to understand planetary movements. Our dependence on electricity has improved most aspects of our modern lives. So we can easily agree that there is freedom in certain dependencies. Take a moment to consider the natural laws of the universe. These are the rules by which all changes occur.

We cannot begin to understand many of these laws, but some we do. Gravity is one we all agree upon. So what about the guy who despite the knowledge of ages insists that he can prevent himself from falling from the sky to the ground? He steps out of a first story window to prove that he won't hit the pavement below, but does. So in defiance he climbs to the second floor of his building and leaps out a window there, only to find that he again plummets to the earth. Now frustrated, he runs to the third story and leaps again, this time breaking his leg. After months of recovery and having supposedly learned his lesson, he finds himself on the ledge of a fourth story window again determined to prove that he can overpower gravity, this time paralyzing himself. He is not very different from the person who is determined to defeat violence with sheer human will power. Despite all that we have learned about ourselves regarding violence, we found that only the willingness to let go of control could consistently confirm our freedom from the incessant habit of its use. It was only by turning our will over on a daily basis that we were able to establish anything like continuous sobriety from violence. But this was just the beginning. Success lies in the remaining Steps. The true test of our willingness was the action required to follow through with Steps 4 through 12. We VAs have found, from experience, that freedom from violent behavior is built on the firm bedrock of willingness to turn our will and lives over to a higher power. Our best expression of this willingness is attending VA Meetings, working these 12 Steps and employing the VA Tools on a daily basis.

It's clear that I had been unknowingly placing my dependence on power and control. When I felt that my well being or my plan was in jeopardy, I resorted to violence as a means of maintaining what I believed to be balance. However, this strategy failed to bring about true balance or any lasting resolution to whatever conflict I applied it. Instead it brought ruin, destruction and severed relations with people. Violence took me further from my true goal of peace and prosperity for myself and others. My loved ones were afraid of me and business partners fled from agreements, not wanting to deal with my behavior or fearing how it would affect the bottom line. So it's safe to say that my dependency on violence as a means of power has failed, and turning to a power greater than violence might be a good start.

Many VAs change the language of Step 3 to fit their particular belief about God or a higher power. Some VAs view a "spiritual awakening" as a psychological and emotional maturing that does not require a "God," but instead a reliance on the fellowship of VA. I have trouble with the language of "greater than myself" since my faith is based on the belief that God and I are one and that in my best form I am carrying out the will of God at each moment. I cannot argue that I often fall short of my highest potential, hence my arrival in Violence Anonymous. It is by putting my power in my false-self/small-self/ego-self that I fall short and forfeit my connection to my God-self. So "A power greater than my false-self or my unhealthy ego" is more appropriate for me. Regardless of the language one uses, the point is the same. We have found ourselves at the bottom and in order to climb out we must lay down our previous beliefs and find a faith that works. If we continue along our violent path, we are surely doomed to more misery. So we begin by turning our will and our lives over to God, as we understand God. The wording of any prayer is optional, the point is that we express sincerity and make an honest attempt at willingness to change. Many VA's begin with the Serenity Prayer.

"God grant me the serenity to accept the things I cannot change, courage to change the things I can and wisdom to know the difference. Thy will and mine be one."

Others prefer this 3rd Step Prayer found in the Big Book of Alcoholics Anonymous.

"God, I offer myself to Thee-to build with me and to do with me as Thou wilt. Relieve me of the bondage of self, that I may better do Thy will. Take away my difficulties, that victory over them may bear witness to those I would help of Thy Power, Thy Love, and Thy Way of Life. May I do Thy will always!"

Some of us found it helpful to take this spiritual step with another VA, a close family member, Sponsor or spiritual advisor. Some found it better to take this Step alone, rather than sharing this delicate moment with someone who might misunderstand. However it is done, as long as we approach Step 3 with an honest and humble heart we find the effects deep and profound.

Exercise 21

In what ways do I need to let go of control?

Exercise 22

How can I use the VA Tools to let go of control?

Step 4

Made a searching and fearless moral inventory of ourselves.

This process is a deep and profound one that can bring up pain and shame that has been hidden for years. We suggest you create the safest environment possible to do this work. Keep in mind that you may feel vulnerable during your 4th Step process. Especially when you are unable to complete your entire inventory in one setting. We VAs have found it very useful to bookend our 4th Step inventory work with a prayer, or contact with another VA, for guidance and protection prior to beginning and upon completion of each inventory session. This helps us avoid the trap of inventorying everyone and everything throughout our day. Many of us use the serenity prayer. "God, grant me serenity to accept the things I cannot change, courage to change the things I can, and wisdom to know the difference."

What is morality? Is it possibly a subjective description of the ethics that we and our society have decided upon? Could it be that each person's moral code is different? This may be why every major religion has tried to lay out a rulebook of moral obligations that one must follow in order to obtain a higher state of consciousness or redemption. We in VA are not here to dictate to you what your moral code should be or what rules you may want to utilize as a guide. We are here to help each other arrest the cycle of violence that we find so habitual and destructive in our lives and to assist in building a bridge back to a life of contribution to one's family and society. If we decide, over time, to align our moral compasses toward a higher good, that's all the better.

So why must we do an inventory at all? Haven't we changed enough by admitting that we have a problem and turning it over to a power greater than violence? Haven't we sacrificed enough by practicing the tools of VA and attending meetings? Haven't we already embarrassed ourselves by telling our stories and admitting that our way of dealing in the world has gone terribly wrong? Must we now humble ourselves further and clean the wounds we so dearly protect? The answer from every recovering VA is a resounding "YES." Abstaining from violent behavior is not enough to ensure that we will continue to resist its power over us. It is our thinking that has gone astray and it is that thinking that we continue to carry with us into our everyday lives. How can we ensure that our thinking will change?

This is the beginning. It is here that we lift the veil of ignorance and begin to understand how we create our own downfall and how we can rise from the ashes of despair to find a life worth living on the other side of violent thought. It is now that we begin to align with an understanding of self.

Most of us know by now, in this world of self-actualization, that our thoughts lead to emotions. Our emotions influence actions. Our actions form our habits. And our habits become our character. But how many of us have really taken stock in the thoughts and emotional baggage that inform our life of its direction? Some of us are scholars and PhDs. Some have accumulated great wealth and power and may even be fighting for lasting social change. Others have spent years in therapy uncovering the inner workings of our minds. At the very least, we are all smart enough to finally arrive at a VA meeting. Yet we all find ourselves in a society of increasing violence and our own behavior has brought humiliation and shame to ourselves, our families and perhaps our businesses. Nearly every serious emotional problem can be seen as a misdirected thought. And now, we find that our greatest asset, our thinking, has become our own crippling mental and physical liability.

In Step 4, we each make a thorough inventory of our assets and liabilities in order to gain a better understanding of what is driving our thinking and the ways we meet our needs. Whether we are working this step as a Victim, Rescuer, or Persecutor, our path to recovery is dependent upon a deeper understanding of our needs, how we go about meeting them and how our approach to meeting our needs has been leading us astray. Let's simplify our list of human needs down to the following six.* You may want to add to this list, but let's use it as a starting point.

Inventory Part One - Six Human Needs

Certainty/Comfort (Safety)

Who doesn't need safety and comfort? Human kind has striven for advancements in the technologies of shelter, running water, electricity and transportation. Our need to know that we can avoid pain, get from home to work in a certain time frame, or that our boss will be happy when we perform well is all driven by our need for safety and comfort. And much of this sense of safety and comfort comes from certainty. Of course there is no absolute certainty, but don't we want to know that we are free from danger, the car will start, the water will flow from the tap, and the currency we use will hold its value? How do we go about creating certainty for ourselves? Do we use power and control to force others to do what we believe will give us the comfort of a chosen outcome? Does our greed for money, sex, or power and our desire to hoard it, supersede the happiness of others? Whether in the local community group or on the world stage, how often have we seen this behavior create resentment, anger and a desire for revenge in others? Do we compromise our integrity by telling that little white lie to manipulate others into coming over to our side? How about telling bald-face lies to accomplish the same end? Do we judge people or cultures to have the comfort of a superior world-view? Which of us hasn't met our need for certainty by saying just the thing we knew would hurt another person? We are sure that we will feel superior in the certainty of knowing we have the power to change another's mood from contentment to despair in a single phrase. We may even be conscious of what we are doing yet we are powerless to stop ourselves. How about the VA who, determined to depend completely on a "stronger" person, convinces others to support them financially? Eventually these protectors (Rescuers) either flee or die, leaving this control addict alone and afraid. Each of these examples finds the VA stuck on the Drama Triangle playing the role of Persecutor, Victim or Rescuer in a fruitless attempt to meet their need for Certainty.

There are positive ways to meet this need as well. Take the VA who, after a slow start of it, begins to understand the power of a fair business deal. He, having learned the hard way by fighting the court battle or the numerous power struggles and sabotages, can now meet his need for financial comfort or security while making it easier for others to do the same. He may have to confront huge fears, but will sleep far sounder in having done so, and will no longer live with the guilt and shame of taking advantage of others by manipulating to meet his need for certainty. Let's take the VA who has come to understand herself well enough to know when she needs some solitude. Knowing that she has in the past met this need by creating an argument, thus frightening others to back off from her space, she now chooses to explain her need for time alone, and takes responsibility for that need while including others in the process. When she becomes aware of her need for space, rather than creating an argument to force others to go away, she can meet her need for certainty by removing herself from the situation. Maybe she'll go on a walk, a drive, read a book or see a film. By doing so, she can be certain that she will remain calmer, and can be sure that her family will be happier than if she had stuck around to pick a fight, in order to create the space she desired.

Exercise 23

Write down the ways you use power and control to meet your need for certainty/comfort.

Exercise 24

Now write the healthy ways you meet your need for certainty/comfort. These will generally create an experience of ease, cooperation, connection and peace.

Uncertainty/Variety.

Paradoxically, at the same time that we need certainty, we also must have uncertainty or variety. We require enough uncertainty to provide spice and adventure in our lives. How many times have we found ourselves bored and needing a change? This is driven by our need for uncertainty. So how do we go about creating uncertainty for ourselves? Do we take unnecessary risks and lose the family fortune? Do we act out against the violence at home by overspending or promiscuous sexual relations because "they deserve it"? Do we create arguments with family, friends or at the sports arena? Or perhaps shout at the stranger in traffic for some violation real or imagined? There are healthy ways to fulfill this need as well, and each of us will define what is healthy for ourselves. Perhaps we surprise our partner or friend with a night on the town, or a trip to that place they always talk about. Spontaneously taking a new route home or a walk in the park could be a beginning. Maybe trying a new hobby or a different recipe is enough to meet our need for uncertainty.

Exercise 25

Write down the ways you use power and control to meet your need for uncertainty/variety.

Exercise 26

Now write the healthy ways you meet your need for uncertainty/variety. These will generally create an experience of ease, cooperation, connection and peace.

Significance

Deep down, we all want to be important. We want our life to have meaning and significance. Who doesn't respond to a "pat on the back" for a job well done? Who doesn't want to feel like they really matter to family, friends or society? Who doesn't enjoy being acknowledged for their efforts? Some of us may not prioritize this as our number one need, but can't we all agree that this need for significance drives our thoughts and our actions? We all want to feel the joy of being special or important. So how do we go about meeting this need? Are we the one who will do something harmful to another to feel significant and powerful in their life? Does our need for significance come out in ways that drive people from us, leaving them feeling smothered and furious? Or do we feel significant when we help someone in the way that they would like to be helped?

Exercise 27

Write down the negative ways that you meet your need for significance. These might create temporary relief, but tend to create long term suffering for you and others.

Exercise 28

Write down the positive ways that you meet your need for significance. These usually require vulnerability, asking for help or being of service in a way that doesn't compromise our other needs.

Connection/Love

We all have a need for love. We want to feel part of a community. We want to be cared for and cared about. However, the way we connect with others is not always for the highest good. Consider the VA who picks fights to feel connected to others, they might feel fulfilled during a good power struggle, thinking that they are finally communicating with their partner. The partner, on the other hand, may feel scared, frustrated, or even persecuted with each interaction. How about the VA who uses resentment for past hurts to be the conduit for connection with others? This person finds themselves wallowing in self-pity and depression as a way of meeting this need. They may spend years slandering others rather than giving love to connect. Both VAs from these examples find themselves trapped on the Drama Triangle, and therefore meet their need for connection in violent ways. Is this the deep connection they really need or a false connection that leaves them isolated and alone? Many prominent human behavior experts of our time agree that we feel love when we give love. We VAs find this to be the absolute truth. Only upon coming to this understanding could we begin to connect to others in a productive way; with a thought, a prayer or an act of generosity. We VAs have found that, without a searching and fearless moral inventory, meeting our need for connection and love in a way that uplifts those around us is still out of reach.

Exercise 29

Write down the negative and positive ways that you meet your need for connection/love.

Let us take an example of how one of us might meet these first four needs with violence. Suppose a man decides that he will rob a convenience store. He pulls his gun as he walks through the door and shouts "everyone on the floor or you're dead." His need for **Uncertainty** is immediately met due to the many outcomes that could follow. He doesn't know if the owner will have a gun behind the counter and he will be shot, or maybe he will be caught by the police and incarcerated. His need for **Significance** is certainly met. There is no doubt that everyone in the store is paying full attention to him as he threatens to shoot them if they don't do exactly what he wants. And he is **Certain** that he is in control of the situation for the moment. He also feels a sense of **Connection** with his victims. This is an extreme example. Each VA is, no doubt, aware, that there are also more subtle ways to use violence to meet these first four needs.

Take the woman who uses shaming comments to persuade others to take care of her. She may think that "educating" someone of their faults is a good way of meeting her need for **Connection.** She believes that if she points out better ways for the other to behave that she will be **Certain** to have her own needs met. This Rescuer sees herself as the Victim in the situation and so justifies her bossy behavior. By playing the role of "the person with all the answers," she feels **Significant.** She also meets her need for **Uncertainty**, since she is unsure whether the other will relent to her pushy ways or if they will react with resistance, or even force.

How about the depressive? This person knows with **Certainty** that if they meet each situation by jumping into the victim role, they will soon feel self-pity and sorrow or possibly even anger. They have trodden this unhappy road many-a-time and know its terrain well. Many VAs have fallen into this class. The depressive can fulfill their need for **Uncertainty** by acting out around different people, never being able to predict how others will respond. Will they come back as a rescuer and attempt to pull our poor depressive VA from the pits of despair? Will they become the persecutor, lashing out in anger and frustration? Perhaps they will remain neutral, unaffected by the depressive's futile attempt to hijack the relationship with this more subtle form of violence. Their need for **Significance** is met by being just enough of a drag to ruffle the feathers of the well-intentioned friend, colleague or family member. This depressive VA, like the convenience store robber, gains **Connection** with others by using "power and control." It took me years to finally admit to myself that I was participating in this form of violence and slowly driving my friends and family mad with my lack of mental control and my ignorance of the effects of my behavior. Of course there are clinical cases of depression that are beyond this description, but for many of us a clear understanding of the Drama Triangle roles and a thorough inventory of our behavior in those roles can be the beginning of a spiritual antidote for depression.

Exercise 30

Take a moment to write down a few examples of how you have used violence to meet your first four needs.

Exercise 31

Write down some examples of how you use non-violence to meet your needs.

According to Marshall Rosenberg, author of Nonviolent Communication, "NVC guides us in reframing how we express ourselves and hear others. Instead of habitual, automatic reactions, our words become conscious responses based firmly on awareness of what we are perceiving, feeling, and wanting. We are led to express ourselves with honesty and clarity, while simultaneously paying others respectful and empathetic attention... As NVC replaces old patterns of defending, withdrawing, or attacking in the face of judgment and criticism, we come to perceive ourselves and others, as well as our intentions and relationships, in a new light. Resistance, defensiveness, and violent reactions are minimized."

What do you do to share your needs honestly with others and ask for their help in meeting your needs in cooperation with theirs?

Growth

The process of developing or maturing, physically, mentally, and spiritually. It's easy to look out into any woods in spring and summer and see that the trees are growing, and those that are not, are dying. It's a simple fact of nature. Where we refuse to grow we begin the process of death. Some VAs may reach

Step Four, the point of an inventory, and proclaim, "I have grown enough! Why should I make a searching and fearless moral inventory of my resentments and fears? Whose business is it, anyway, my sexual conduct? I'm not interested in understanding needs. This is where I put my foot down!" Many before this VA have reached the same conclusion and have needed to stop and rest. The important point here is to not let this rest become the beginning of the end. When growth seems impossible, the best plan of action is to rely upon a source that is greater than our resistance to growing. Only a power greater than my violent behavior could shine the light in the pit of despair that would lead me from hell to a life of contribution. Growth is an inevitable need. It is up to each VA to decide if we will grow toward violent behavior or toward the peace of mind of the following Steps.

Exercise 32

Write down the ways you may be growing toward violence. How do you meet your own needs at the expense of others?

Exercise 33

Write down the ways you meet your need for growth by creating joy and peace for yourself and others.

Contribution

The desire to contribute something of value, to help others, to leave the world a better place than we found it, is in all of us. Many VAs make wonderful contributions to society, and yet, behind closed doors we torment our families and frighten our friends. We commit to uplifting the public while contributing to undermine the trust of our children or parents. We must begin to realize how our insecurities and fears are allowing us to meet our needs in negative ways. Perhaps we may find it useful to practice with other VAs in Violence Anonymous meetings or by sharing our process with a sponsor. Simply by honestly and humbly taking stock in ourselves we begin the journey of turning the poison of our shortcomings into medicine for a healthy and prosperous life. Our need for contribution can be met by bringing others into the intimate and truthful world we create.

My friend Doug likes to buy people groceries, to meet his need for contribution. He will pick a stranger in the line at the grocer and simply give the cashier the money for their bill. One might think that he is from a privileged background and that he just has money to burn, but he grew up in the same small town as I. As boys we would scrounge for coins in change slots of Coke machines. I often think of him when I need inspiration for acting with generosity. When I act in the same manner I understand a true sense of power.

Exercise 34

Write down the ways you resist contributing to the wellbeing of others.

Exercise 35

Write down the positive ways that you meet your need for contribution.

Resistance

Let's consider the newcomer who is offended by the idea of an inventory. They may think, "Now that I am abstinent, my good nature will surely return and there is no need for me to take stock in these so-called shortcomings." How is the sponsor of this type of VA going to help them at all? Perhaps the sponsor has a bit of experience with having an overblown ego or unconsciously protecting our pain and trauma. Likely, they too had to confront the pride that kept them in the throws of a violent mind. After all, who likes to endure the pain of having to change, especially when it means confronting guilt and shame from our past behavior? What violence addict wakes up in the morning saying, "Gee I can't wait to feel the embarrassment of coming to terms with the person I have become"? Many have come to this threshold, but only the truly courageous have passed over to the other side. Those of us who did carry on had reached a bottom so severe that we could not turn back. Perhaps this VA has not had enough of the agony that violence has caused the rest of us. Perhaps it's time for them to go back to their old ways and endure a few more years of attempting to control people, places and situations in times of stress. Perhaps a jail sentence or the death of someone is the only thing that will awaken this type of newcomer to the truth about their addiction to violence. At this point the sponsor must not pass judgment, but let go as graciously as possible, for there is no room for power struggle here. Each person must come to this Step of their own accord.

At the thought of making a searching and fearless moral inventory, the Victim may scream out, "It's them that need to do the inventory! They are the abuser and I am innocent." This may be true in some cases, like the person who was forced to endure abuses, the refugee fleeing someone else's war or the person who has endured systemic persecution. Any time violence is used against another it is a very serious situation that requires time, empathy, and compassion to find healing. Those cases aside, if a VA is truly honest with themselves, most will admit that it takes two to tango. It has been my experience that when I play the victim I am acting out the flip side of the same coin that the perpetrator or rescuer is on. In other words, simply believing myself to be a victim can be a violent act. I have the power to change by admitting my part. The sponsor of the VA who clings to the Victim role will want to try and find a chink in the armor of their ego. They will do this by relating to how they once believed the same and how they were able to walk through the fear and find a new and better way of life; a life free from resentment, self-pity and unwarranted fear; a life where the idea of blame is a thing of the past and where taking responsibility for one's own thoughts and actions becomes second nature. The sponsor may remind the newcomer that when we are stuck in the Victim role, we are usually triggered. Processing this trigger and neutralizing the original trauma will allow this VA to proceed. With practice this process becomes easier and the gift of humility follows soon after.

What about the Rescuer who feels codependent to violent people? This VA may find it difficult to see their part in the cycle of violence. To them, they are simply reacting to the aggressor and therefore really have no responsibility in the matter. This Violence Addict understands that something must shift, but thinks that it is the other who must change in order for them to be happy and feel safe. This Rescuer finds themselves in the same situation as the Victim. They must learn to let go of the idea that they are innocent and come to terms with the harsh reality that they are dependent on violence. They are co-creating the situations that render them helpless and by making a fearless and thorough moral inventory they, too, can find freedom from the false pride of power and control. Each VA will have to determine for themselves their own deficits.

Often we VAs may find someone's behavior upsetting. This may be an indication that we behave in a similar fashion. In other words, "You spot it, you got it." This little piece of knowledge can shift irritating situations into gifts of much needed clarity about ourselves. Once we VAs can harness our own behavior, that mirror in others is no longer a source of pain. So how do we start? Whether one would call it a moral inventory, a list of character defects, an excavation of destructive habits, or taking stock of one's negative thought patterns, the point is to begin in bending our attention from blame to personal responsibility.

Inventory Part Two – 7 Deadly Sins

Now that we have taken a first look at how we meet our needs in violent and non-violent ways and some of the ways we allow violence to talk us out of continuing on, how do we continue this inventory? What questions must we ask ourselves and how do we answer them?

Many VA Sponsors will begin with presenting a list of the 7 deadly sins: Pride, Greed, Lust, Anger, Gluttony, Envy and Sloth. Each VA may want to examine how fear, guilt, and shame drive them to overcompensate with these behaviors.

Exercise 36

Make a list of how your thoughts, actions and behaviors are influenced by the 7 deadly sins.

Pride

Greed

Lust

Anger

Gluttony

Envy

Sloth

Inventory Part Three – Resentments, Fears, and Sexual Conduct

Our Sponsors encourage us to document our Resentments, Fears and Sexual Conduct. Taking into consideration our thoughts that keep us trapped on the Drama Triangle and stuck in the cycle of violence. First, let's define the meaning of each column title so we can easily follow through with the final stage of our inventory.

Person, Place, Thing or Situation that I Resent or Fear.

Exercise 37

Write down who or what you resent or fear and why.

What role on the Drama Triangle am I playing?

Exercise 38

Write down Victim, Rescuer, or Persecutor and any other information that will help you understand what role you are playing on the Drama Triangle.

What Needs are affected?

Exercise 39

List any of your needs that are being affected. Many find it simpler to group our needs into the 6 basic human needs discussed earlier.

What is the pattern/handle?

Exercise 40

How do I see this pattern repeating in my life? How is this experience similar to other experiences from my past? What image of this experience can I use to process the trigger and neutralize the original trauma that started this pattern? In Step 5, the Sponsor will help the Sponsee understand and recognize the handles (common threads that reveal the pattern) so these traumas can be neutralized in Steps 6 and 7.

Example:

Resentments

Person, Place, Thing or Situation that I Resent.	What role on the Drama Triangle am I playing?	What Needs are affected?	What is the Pattern /Handle?
Dad reneged on paying for college	Victim	Support (Safety/Certainty), Respect (Significance)	I often find myself in situations where I don't trust others to do what they say they will do.
Stan acts ungrateful, moans and complains	Persecutor – I lose my cool and yell at him.	Safety/Certainty, Respect (Significance), Connection – We connect by fighting	I'm easily upset by depressive types.
Susan cut	Rescuer – I	Love/Connect	I can think of

Person, Place, Thing or Situation that I Resent.	What role on the Drama Triangle am I playing?	What Needs are affected?	What is the Pattern /Handle?
me out of the relationship and painted herself as the victim.	just kept giving and giving without meeting my own needs. Victim – I feel hurt by her actions	ion, Feeling Special (Significance), Safety/Certain ty	three other times I've given and given and given and not gotten what I needed in return.

Fears

Person, Place, Thing or Situation that I Fear.	What role on the Drama Triangle am I playing?	What Needs are affected?	What is the Pattern /Handle?
I will fail at earning more than I need	Victim – when I'm looking for a hand out or for someone to save me, Persecutor - When I	Financial Security (Safety/Certai nty), Self-Respect (Significance), Contribution – I want to provide for	I'm afraid to open bills. I often find myself scraping by and not having enough

Person, Place, Thing or Situation that I Fear.	What role on the Drama Triangle am I playing?	What Needs are affected?	What is the Pattern /Handle?
	snap at people.	my family.	money.
If I let my child learn at their own pace he will fail.	Victim – I get embarrassed when he gets behind. Rescuer – I try to "Educate" him when he doesn't want my help. Persecutor – I lose my patience and boss him around.	Safety/Certainty, Respect (Significance), Connection – I connect with him by arguing, trying to "educate" him or rejecting him.	I'm very uncomfortable when people are slow or don't work at my pace. I'm often impatient. My mom treated me this way.
My family will leave me	Rescuer – I just kept giving and giving without meeting my own needs Victim – I	Love/Connection, Feeling Special (Significance), Safety/Certainty	My dad traveled a lot and was often gone. I felt sad all the time. This feels the same.

Person, Place, Thing or Situation that I Fear.	What role on the Drama Triangle am I playing?	What Needs are affected?	What is the Pattern /Handle?
	feel abandoned		
Dad reneged on paying for college	Victim	Support (Safety/Certainty), Respect (Significance)	I often find myself in situations where I don't trust others to do what they say they will do.
Stan acts ungrateful, moans and complains	Persecutor – I lose my cool and yell at him.	Safety/Certainty, Respect (Significance), Connection – We connect by fighting	I'm easily upset by depressive types.
Susan cut me out of the relationship and painted herself as the victim.	Rescuer – I just kept giving and giving without meeting my own needs. Victim – I feel hurt by her actions.	Love/Connection, Feeling Special (Significance), Safety/Certainty	I can think of three other times I've given and given and given and not gotten what I needed in return.

Sexual Conduct

Write down who you hurt and what happened.

Example:

Sexual Conduct.	What role on the Drama Triangle am I playing?	What Needs are affected?	What is the Pattern /Handle?
I cheated on my partner	Victim – I made out that she was withholding sex from me. Persecutor – I decided to show her how much pain I was in by hurting her. Then I lied about it.	Self-Respect (Significance), Love and Connection,	I felt sexually frustrated and thought "To hell with her!" Instead of clearly asking for my needs to be met. I often want to hurt people who I think are hurting me.

Sexual Conduct.	What role on the Drama Triangle am I playing?	What Needs are affected?	What is the Pattern /Handle?
I withheld love and affection from my partner.	Victim – I wasn't getting what I wanted. Persecutor – I withheld sex to have power over my partner.	Safety/Certainty, Respect (Significance), Love and Connection, Uncertainty/Variety – I wasn't sure if they would argue with me or submit.	I use seduction or withhold affection to control others.

However we go about making a searching and fearless moral inventory we rely on the principle of thoroughness. This is the first tangible proof of our decision to turn our will and our lives over to God as we understand God.

Exercise 41

Write Part Three of your inventory.

Step 5

Admitted to God, to ourselves and to another human being the exact nature of our wrongs.

Few Steps are harder to take than Step 5. This is the tipping point. Many VAs have asked, "Will I hold onto my secrets and keep myself isolated from God and others or will I trust this program and let go of the darkened forest of my shame and guilt into the light?" Now that we have mustered the courage to put our thorough inventory to paper, we must consider if we are truly willing to share it with God and another human being. Some have found it easy to share with God. "Ok God, you heard me write down my 4th Step, now you know. Isn't that enough?" Most have found it harder to feel the embarrassment of admitting these intimate and isolating secrets with another person. If we really want to clean house we must bear our souls with another so that we may liberate ourselves from the grip of shame that has kept us bound to violent thought and action. We have tried anonymous confession and have not had the same result as a face-to-face admission of our gravest behaviors.

Without an overwhelming desire to change, and faith in a power greater than violent behavior, we are frozen in the grips of the cycle of violence that has dominated our behavior for as long as we can recall. Many VAs have derailed the train at this station, heading back down the tracks of destructive behavior. Others, who hesitated, have struggled with periodic relapse until they were sincerely ready to clean house. But those who are willing to experience the true meaning of humility are ready to take this Step by sharing their burden of guilt and shame with God and another human being.

Open expression is the critical step in breaking our isolation. Exposing those rattling bones lying in our closets to another human being is the only path to true liberation from their shameful grip on us. This fact we have derived from experience. We must talk to someone else. It is perhaps the most imperative suggestion we have shared thus far. It's easy to confess what people already know about us, but what about the fear of exposing the truly humiliating secrets? Many of us have vowed to take those to the grave. Skimping at this moment has proven perilous to those who seek real freedom. Holding back on Step 5 has created more grief to our friends in recovery than any other fearful act. We must summon the resolve of lonely warriors who fight without allies for what we know is a cause greater than any other. Irony reveals to us that, by mustering such courage and holding nothing back, we find we have more allies than ever before, and our lives bloom into those intimate visions we have only dared see in our most private and hope filled dreams.

Our society is riddled with potential VAs who, rather than examine their own defects, find it more enjoyable to project their darkest fears onto friends, family and society. We should not judge them too harshly, since we too have been those people and only by sheer grace do we stand ready to change. To them we simply say that our weakness has also rendered us powerless over the obsession to declare the sins of others, and in the end each person must confess their own.

Confession has been a fundamental pillar of spiritual growth since ancient times. Every major spiritual movement and religion has utilized its power to heal. Therapists and psychiatrists help people empower themselves by assessing their own behavior and admitting their faults to a trusted advisor. It's common knowledge today that the emotional relief of confessing something is equal to physically taking off an unnecessarily heavy coat. But for VAs this act of faith is the doorway we must walk through in order to experience a true change in our behavior. This is the portal that leads from the embarrassing world of broken relationships, ruined business deals and unnecessary wars to the world of honorable action, mutual respect and cooperation with our friends, families and neighbors. It is by sharing our fears, resentments, and destructive behaviors that we increase our odds of abstaining from the throws of violent thinking and lead ourselves out of victimhood, rescuer-ville, and persecution-alley. Sharing these embarrassments with another human being breaks the spell of our destructive obsessions and grants us humility to carry on, one day at a time. VAs know from experience that the grace of God cannot expel our addiction to power and control until we are willing to try this.

Many VAs may ask, "What pleasure will I gain from enduring the pain of full disclosure with God and another human being? What benefit could there possibly be from humbling myself?" For one thing, that terrible feeling of isolation slips away. VAs, without exception, are tortured by loneliness. Even before our addiction to power and control brought us to our knees, we began to feel cut off. Nearly all of us suffered from the belief that we didn't quite fit in. Either we were shy and submissive, fearing that we would be attacked and controlled, or we were boisterous and loud, banging through life to get the attention and care we craved, but only occasionally succeeding at meeting our needs in cooperation with others. There was always that hidden barrier that kept us from a real and lasting connection with other people. We could see what we wanted, but were unable to break through the invisible force field that imprisoned us. It was our violent thinking that kept us repeating the same actions and expecting different results. It is that very thinking that must change for us to overcome the deafening loneliness that holds us hostage.

When we reached VA, for the first time in our lives we found others like us, who understood our woes. At first this was enough, but in time we found the same social issues that kept us lonely and isolated re-emerged. The intimacy, love and connection we craved still eluded us. Step 5, sharing with another and listening to another do the same, was the answer. This is the next step toward true kinship with God as we understood God. By proceeding with Step 5, we find freedom from the belief that we don't fit in. The desire to cut people out of our lives slips away, as does the shame of having been cut out by others.

Step Five is the seed to the sapling of forgiveness. While working with our sponsors or spiritual advisers on this step, we begin to get a glimpse of how it feels to forgive ourselves and others. We experience the relief of knowing that we could be forgiven, no matter how horrible our violent behavior had become. Whether we had found "false power" as rescuer, perpetrator, or victim, we VAs who have crossed this threshold can attest that, if properly tended by the following steps, this sapling of forgiveness blooms into a solid oak.

The Fourth Step gives us a look into honesty and tolerance, the fifth grants us humility. Alcoholics Anonymous was the first 12 Step program. In the 1930's, early recovering alcoholics laid a foundation for all 12 Step programs to follow. Violence Anonymous was born from that foundation. The founder of AA, writes about humility in this way: "It amounts to a clear recognition of what and who we really are, followed by a sincere attempt to become what we could be." We all found that we are riddled with self-pity, fear and anger. It was not easy to muster the courage to put these deficiencies to paper in Step Four, but awareness alone will not cultivate the humility that is necessary to recover. That awareness must be fused together with action, that action is sharing our inventory with God and another human being.

This brings us to the VA who declares, "Why can't God just take these problems of fear and guilt? If there is an all-knowing presence, doesn't it already know what I think and feel? Surely my thinking will just be corrected without having to humiliate myself in front of another." To this line of thinking, a sponsor's reply might be, "How has that worked so far?" If liberation from the Drama Triangle is what you seek, honest admission to another human being, in the presence of your higher power, is the key to the exit hatch.

Our objectivity toward our own thinking has become skewed. We need help in untangling our constructive thinking from our violent thinking. Even great spiritual advisors have spiritual advisors. How many times has history witnessed wars initiated by someone who claims to have heard the "voice of God"? Probably best for us VAs to check our thinking with someone else in recovery. This way we can learn to trust another and experience humility, by taking suggestions from a friend who has experience with overcoming violent thinking and behavior.

It occurred to me, while working Step 5, that an expert might know more than I. If you are like me, you may be skeptical of authority due to a violent past. How do I know that I'm choosing someone who has my best interest in mind? How can I be sure that I'm not walking into another emotional trap, where I give and give, never to have my needs met? This is where it's important for every VA to understand that a sponsor is not a savior, but a guide to provide empathy and a non-judgmental ear. Although not infallible, a sponsor is rarely surprised by the past actions of another VA. Despite the differences in the path, all of us have found our way to complete defeat and then climbed from the pit of despair to solid ground, by relying on the power of Violence Anonymous, the 12 Steps and the companionship of others who share our experience.

Our next action is to find the person with whom we will share our Step 5. This is important, as we will be sharing very intimate secrets. Some of which we had sworn to take to our graves. Obviously, we will be looking for someone whose experience may be similar to our own. Maybe even someone who, in addition to arresting their violent behavior, has overcome other serious difficulties like ours. If your sponsor fits the bill, all the better, since they already have insight into your story.

Perhaps you may decide upon sharing your 5th Step with a member of the clergy, or a trusted therapist. This can be equally powerful. For some, a complete stranger will do. The point is to complete Step 5, avoiding any excuse to hold yourself back from experiencing the relief of sharing your shame with God and another human being. The real test is our willingness to completely confide, leaving no stone unturned. Even when you've found the right person it may take great resolve to approach them. Do not be thwarted by rejection, instead practice persistence until you are able to find someone willing to hear your 5th Step. Once face to face, you may find this process becomes easier and the anxiety that preceded this step will be replaced with relief and a connection to God that is deep and profound. At some point your sponsor may wish to share something about their own story, in the interest of providing empathy and relief.

Step 5 begins the process of re-associating the mind of the VA, from confiding equals pain to confiding equals pleasure and relief. It points us toward truth and honesty as the spiritual foundation for our recovery. Humility has replaced humiliation as our greatest ally and has revealed itself as the key to our success in building a new life. A new life whose road map is found in Steps 6 through 12.

Step 6

Were entirely ready to have God remove all these defects of character.

So far, we VAs have ventured well beyond the boundaries of our old way of living. We have shed many of the shackles that accompany the life of a persecutor, rescuer, and victim. We have examined and admitted much of our past and have begun the journey toward a life of happiness free from the bonds of violent thought and action. We have begun to develop a new character based on the integrity of a "Higher Power" rather than the weakness of "power and control." This is where the VA must begin again, and each of us must decide to venture from the wilderness of self-centeredness and into the world of a better life for ourselves, our communities and society. A "God-centered" existence.

To many, whether or not God can do for us what we could not do for ourselves, is a theory that can be debated, but ask any VA who has had the courage to take Steps 1 through 5 and they will tell you, without hesitation, that this is an undisputed fact. Regardless of how a VA may define God, each of us has found relief from the obsession of living on the Drama Triangle. We no longer hope to meet our needs through violent measures. Whether one acted primarily as a rescuer, using the more subtle forms of violent behavior to look like the "good person" while controlling others, or a victim turned persecutor who found themselves in prison for any number of more obviously violent actions, we have been granted a perfect release from using violence to meet our needs. You might hear a VA saying:

"When I arrived in VA, I was scared and exhausted by violence. No human power could restore me to sanity. No education, no resolution, no attempt by family, friends, clergy or officers of the law had prevented my addiction to violence. I simply could not stop. When I became willing to clean my house and asked a higher power to remove my obsession, my desire to use power over people and situations was replaced by the satisfaction of using non-violence to meet my needs, one day at a time."

By now each of us has become "entirely ready" to have God remove the insanity of violence from our DNA. When men, women, and children create enough discord to experience extreme unhappiness, society might view that as insane. The addict to power and control will repeat this behavior over and over hoping to derive the same joy and false power it gave us in the beginning, only to find ourselves creating intolerable and unnecessary agony. Having gone past the point of secretly enjoying the chaos that we create, the violence addict has become bent on self-destruction. Now humbled by the terrific pain of our violent thinking, many VAs wake up to the fact that we are dependent on strategies that will never completely meet our needs.

Each human being has natural desires. Oxford's thesaurus gives us these synonyms:

wish, want, aspiration, fancy, inclination, impulse; yearning, longing, craving, hankering, hunger; eagerness, enthusiasm, determination; informal yen, itch, jones.

Perhaps what is important here is to notice where these desires of ours have begun to dominate our thinking in negative ways. We VAs can't possibly expect complete elimination of desires. Our goal is the state of being unattached to those desires. When attachment warps our thinking to the point of blind willfulness, that is the climax of our departure from any real and lasting connection with ourselves and God. Our distance from such a connection is the measure of our "character defects".

It is our experience in VA, that only through repeated victories over these defects and a consistent change in behavior, do we find a real and lasting transformation of character. Plainly put, the true warrior lives a God centered life. So Step 6 "Were entirely ready..." is how we describe our most sincere attitude in beginning this lifetime work. Do we expect perfection? Hardly. We strive for consistent improvement. Patience is imperative, "Entirely ready" is our strength.

But how many have this degree of readiness? Many of us feel that we are faking the desire to let go absolutely. Here we say, "Yes! Act as if you are ready until your mind comes along for the ride." We have found it easier to "act our way into new thinking" than to "think our way into new acting." Without fail, we must exercise faith. In doing so, we find ourselves on the right track to becoming entirely ready to have these defects of character removed.

It's easy for someone who has come this far in recovering from the grips of an addiction to power and control to see the benefits in letting go of their more glaring character defects. Who wants to be angry enough to murder, greedy enough to steal, lustful enough to rape, proud enough to be called a braggart or gluttonous enough to ruin their own health? Who, when agonized by the chronic pain of envy or paralyzed by sloth, wouldn't want to feel the relief of a release from their powerful spell? It's easy to see how these are extreme victim states of mind. By now any VA who has worked the first 5 Steps can surely agree that the "Victim mindset" has dominated our thinking and led us to the brink of destruction.

But what about the more subtle character defects? What about those thoughts, actions and behaviors that gnaw at us in the corners of our mind? The ones that haven't quite brought us to our knees, the one's we believe that others haven't seen yet. "They are our little secrets," we tell ourselves. "They cause no one harm." I'll just hang on to this a bit longer. Haven't we all found ourselves in this VA's shoes? A wise sponsor once told me, "If it takes up space in your mind, it should probably go to

God." Based on my experience, he was right. By turning such matters over to God, I felt relief from the guilt and shame of compromising my own integrity and, to my surprise, my friends, family and business associates noticed the difference. The addict is usually the last to see what others have sensed for months or even years.

And what about those defects that we simply cannot see? Here we ask God to point us in the right direction. We ask to have the willingness to trust our fellow VAs, our friends and family. They often identify flaws in our strategies for meeting our needs long before we see them ourselves. It was during Step 6 that I made a conscious decision to believe my wife when she claimed I was behaving gruffly. I realized that this was a person I love. That she was brave enough to give me some information that could make our lives happier and that she was not trying to hurt me. Until this point in my recovery, I was unable to believe that people had my best interest at heart. In the past, I had been abused and hurt by those I trusted and that was how I chose to see the whole world. I was the victim and the world was a perpetrator. My only means of protection was to rescue or persecute so I could control them before they hurt me. Only by turning that belief over to a power greater than my current thinking, could I find relief from the painful grip of my addiction to violence. Having crossed that bridge, I was able to admit, "OK, if I'm honest with myself, I know when she is telling the truth. She may not be perfect and she has behaved in violent ways in the past, but she is a good person who loves me and is trying to work on her own issues. I can trust myself to know when she is correct." Many VAs, by the time they have reached this Step, have surrounded themselves with people they can trust. We found many of these people in the fellowship of Violence Anonymous. Now we must trust God enough to admit it.

"Were entirely ready to have God remove all these defects of character" requires us to commence with closer examination of our so-called defects. Those thoughts, actions, and behaviors that keep us from a consistent commune with a power greater than violence. At this stage of our recovery, many VAs become aware of what we call low-level or mild triggers. Those triggers that might not set us off into a melt-down, but instead color our moods and thinking in more subtle ways. These low-level triggers often reveal themselves as depression, grumpiness, moodiness, and retreating into our caves. We begin to see more clearly that when we are feeling even mildly resentful, sad, angry, hurt, betrayed, anxious, depressed, guilty, etc., we are experiencing a low-level trigger and are living on the Drama Triangle.

Here are some examples of behaviors early VA members discovered in Step 6. We use these as guides to tell us when we are triggered and on the Drama Triangle. When we find ourselves in these states it is imperative that we process the triggers that keep us stuck in these violent roles so that we can free ourselves.

These are condensed versions of what can be found in Signs of Victimhood by Lynne Forrest.

Signs of Victimhood

1. Emotional misery

When we experience emotional misery we might be in victimhood. Thinking like a victim creates negative emotions. When we are feeling resentful, angry, hurt, betrayed, anxious, depressed, guilty, ashamed, or other negative emotions, it is likely that we are playing the victim role on the Drama Triangle.

2. Whining and complaining

When we whine or complain mentally or verbally, we are seeing and judging life through the eyes of a victim. Some examples are "Life is not fair," "I'm being mistreated," or "It shouldn't be this way."

3. Judgmental thinking

Making judgments about ourselves or others could be a sign that we are on the Drama Triangle. These judgments are more charged than a simple discernment.

4. Using victim vocabulary

"I can't handle it." "I'll show them." Or "It's not fair…"

5. Constant Melodrama

Constant melodrama is an indicator that we are in victim consciousness. One example is when we seek to be "right" over being at peace.

6.   Comparing ourselves in critical ways

Comparing is a form of judgmental thinking. When we are in a state of victimhood we critically compare ourselves with others. "Why should I even try, I'll never be as good as them." "They are stupid." "I'm bad."

7.   Blaming people, places, things and situations

Anytime we blame something outside of ourselves for our internal experience we are acting as victims.

Exercise 42

How do you see Signs of Victimhood in your own thinking?

Example - *Emotional misery - guilt:*

I feel guilty when I can't rescue my child or partner from his or her triggered state. That guilt drives me to perpetuate the problem. I feel guilty when I feel sexually aroused. I can acknowledge that guilt to my higher power.

Example – Whining and complaining:

I complain about my boss. The truth is I feel hurt when my boss doesn't give me the respect I think I deserve. I could use Nonviolent Communication to express my need and ask for help in meeting that need, rather than feel hurt that he doesn't read my mind and give me what I want.

Write your examples.

Seven Deadly Sins

Exercise 43

Examine your 7 deadly sins list. How are they blocking you from meeting your needs in healthy ways?

1. **Pride**

   Example – I use pride to think that I am somehow superior in intellect and that people need my advice, whether they are asking for it or not. This keeps me from meeting my need for connection in a healthy way. My pride keeps me blind to how much I truly rescue or secretly hope to be rescued. This false sense of security blocks me from truly feeling safe.

2. **Greed**

   Example - Greed has influenced me to use credit cards or take loans to meet my financial commitments and to spend more than I earn. Greed has led me to mislead people and trick them into giving me money. Greed had led me to commit crimes.

3. **Lust**

   Example - When my spouse is not available sexually, I take it personally and use fantasy/pornography/prostitution or distance myself emotionally. I falsely believe this creates safety for me. I also believe it meets my need for comfort and love. Afterwards I feel ashamed or unsatisfied. I am afraid that I will never be able to ask for what I need without appearing selfish.

4. **Anger**

   Example – I use anger to intimidate others into changing so I feel safe. I use anger to cover up my sadness.

5. **Gluttony**

   Example - When I'm triggered I overindulge in food, sex, and other activities. Because I'm triggered I can't find healthy moderation or balance.

6. **Envy**

   Example - I feel envy toward people who know how to get what they want and need. It's easier to envy them than to learn how to get my needs met in a healthy way.

7. **Sloth**

   Example - I have been slothful around meeting my financial, romantic, sexual, emotional, physical needs. I have been lazy in my earning habits and have relied on the rescue to make my dreams come true. "If I could get a big whacking wad of cash everything will be OK." Sloth keeps me undisciplined and seeking the rescue, rather than admitting that I see myself as a victim who wants to be rescued?

Write your examples

Using Leverage

Leverage Exercise

Now let's create some leverage to change our behavior in these areas. If we can associate more pain with continuing the behavior and more pleasure with changing, then it is easier to create healthier thoughts, actions, and habits.

For each sign of victimhood that you have listed, write what you will lose if you continue to use that strategy to meet your needs. What might the bottom look like with each strategy?

1. Emotional misery

> Example - If I continue to feel guilty for every little thing, I may repeatedly create unnecessary drama in my relationships at home and work. My life may become smaller and smaller as I push people further away. I may miss out on business deals and satisfying romance because of my inability to own my true power. I may let those shaming things I was told in the past continue to be my reality and I may lose out on achieving my dreams in life.

Write your answers

2. Whining and complaining

> Example – If I continue to feel hurt when my boss doesn't act as I wish him to, I may repeatedly see myself as a victim and eventually slip into the role of persecutor

by saying or doing something cruel and hurtful. This could result in my losing my position or favor in the organization. My world will speed along the track of seeing myself as a victim in work situations and I may continue to attract people who abuse me.

Write your answers

3.   Judgmental thinking

Write your answers

4.   Using victim vocabulary

Write your answers

5. Constant Melodrama

Write your answers

6. Comparing ourselves in critical ways

Write your answers

7. Blaming others

Write your answers

For each character defect that you have listed, write what you will lose if you continue to use that strategy to meet your needs. What might the bottom look like with each strategy?

Seven Deadly Sins

1.   Pride

Write your answers

2.   Greed

Write your answers

3.   Lust

Example - If I continue use sexual acting out, I'm afraid I will make it harder and harder to ask for my needs from my partner. I may begin to isolate in order to hide my secret and I may become primarily concerned with secretly meeting my sexual needs. My lust may increase to more perverse acting out, and I may be discovered and publicly embarrassed.

Write your answers

3.   Anger

Write your answers

4. Gluttony

Write your answers

5. Envy

Write your answers

6. Sloth

Write your answers

Exercise 44

Write down what will you gain by letting go of each behavior? What would serenity look like?

1. Emotional misery

> Example - By turning my guilt over to a power greater than my desire to feel guilty, I can free myself from the bondage of this habitual false response to life situations. I will create the self-esteem to act with confidence in work and romantic situations. I will allow myself to

enjoy success and own my true power as a loving human being.

Write your answers

2. Whining and complaining

Example - If I give God my willingness to feel hurt, when my boss or anyone else fails to meet my expectations of how they should act, I can free myself from this perpetual state of victim-hood. I can take responsibility in meeting my needs, by using Nonviolent Communication. I can create a life where I live in a state of gratitude for what I do receive from people and I make it easy for them to help me meet my own needs.

Write your answers

3. Judgmental thinking

Write your answers

4.   Using victim vocabulary

Write your answers

5.   Constant Melodrama

Write your answers

6.   Comparing ourselves in critical ways

Write your answers

7.   Blaming others

Write your answers

Seven Deadly Sins

1.   Pride

Write your answers

2.   Greed

Write your answers

3. Lust

> Example - If I am willing to let go of the character defect of lust, I may find new and healthy ways of meeting my sexual needs. I may begin to build a strong sexual relationship where both partners are satisfied and desire each other more frequently. I may be able to experience not only meeting my physical needs, but also my spiritual and emotional needs at the same time.

Write your answers

3.   Anger

Write your answers

4. Gluttony

Write your answers

5. Envy

Write your answers

6. Sloth

Write your answers

What we VAs suggest now is a closer examination of our needs, and which desires support those needs. This gives us a clearer view of how our thoughts and desires may be leading us astray and lays the foundation for thinking that lends itself to true power. The power of being in line with God's will for us.

In Step 4 we made a searching and fearless moral inventory of ourselves. Here we put our needs to paper. Now in Step 6 we examine how we meet these needs. There are as many ways to do this as there are people in Violence Anonymous, so choose a way that best suits you. Here is an example of one way:

Exercise 45

Examine your needs list from Step 4 and write any new needs that you have discovered in these 6 categories. What positive ways can we go about meeting these needs? For example, instead of control, how do you use enthusiasm, determination, eagerness or joy?

Certainty/Comfort

Uncertainty/Variety

Significance

Connection/Love

Growth

What would my life look like if I met all my needs in positive ways?

Once we have compiled our list, and our consciousness begins to catch the scent of these more mild and insidious habits, we embark upon the hunt for correct thinking. It is at this point that we are able to consciously measure our willingness to live the God-centered life of being present.

Some of us have found a few tools helpful in exercising our willingness to let go of our negative views. These are ways that we have broken the pattern of victim thinking. A wise woman once told me a prayer that has worked wonders in my quest for happiness. I have used this prayer thousands of times to remove myself from the Drama Triangle and energetically disconnect from others who are triggered.

"God, I pray to find in you what I may be looking for in this person, place or thing. I pray that this person, place or thing finds in you, what they may be looking for in me."

If this prayer is not for you, consider an alternative. Another tool is changing location, removing ourselves from a victim state by leaving the room and taking a walk. A friend of VA once said, "If you want to change your mind, change your environment." This is a way to employ the tool, change attention. How many of us have found that a good change of scenery has assisted us in forgetting our woes and focused us on something more productive? For the tougher jobs we may turn to our new positive anchors from Step 2.

Some of us may think, "But I'm simply denying the truth by changing my attention to a more positive state. I'm faking it." To this, a sponsor or fellow VA may reply with a simple question, "Where did that 'truth,' as you call it, get you so far?" If the answer is the same as ours (to the painful rock bottom of violent behavior), then you might just benefit from our newfound oasis, in the desert of negative "victim" thinking. Why not empower yourself to a state of thinking that includes the presence of God, as we understand God, and allow for more creative responses than that of a victim, rescuer or persecutor?

In Step 6 we become better acquainted with the tool of Nonviolent Communication. Many of our conflicts, as violence addicts, stem from our inability to communicate without judging others. By learning Nonviolent Communication and utilizing this tool in our daily conversations we not only become better at clarifying our own needs and the feelings that stem from our thoughts about those needs, but we also learn how to listen for the feelings and needs of others, regardless of how those people speak. For many VAs, the application of Nonviolent Communication becomes more evident and necessary in this Step. As we tune in to the more subtle attributes of our orientation to conflict, by examining our character defects, we find that a new communication style becomes necessary to our continued recovery.

Along with this heightened awareness of our propensity for conflict we began to understand our low-level triggers. By now, extreme triggers or high-level triggers are pretty easily identified. Our sponsors will tell us, "Our recovery is not an immediate job where we come into VA and simply stop triggering, like you would stop drinking or taking drugs. Instead, our brand of recovery consists of stumbling into triggers and being willing to look more deeply into the traumas buried under each trigger." So by the time we have reached Step 6, we have become accustomed to triggering, removing ourselves from the situation without blaming the other person, changing our state by processing the trigger, and healing by bringing our minds into a state of neutrality. Simply put, we now have experience walking out of the fog of "Victim thinking." Since we have this experience, we can now easily identify an extreme trigger in ourselves and in others. In Step 6, we begin to tune into the subtlety of the low-level trigger. These triggers are more akin to the perpetual bad mood or the grumpy spell. We may not be over-reacting as we did before, but we find ourselves participating in the mindset of the ill-tempered, moody, cranky, sullen, and cross. In dealing with low-level triggers our sponsors will recommend applying the same process. Identify the trauma and process it using our chosen form of trauma neutralization. When we are feeling resentful, angry, hurt, betrayed, anxious, depressed, guilty, ashamed, etc., we are playing the victim role on the Drama Triangle. Step 6 encourages us to become entirely ready to have God remove these defects of character.

What about those character defects that despite our best efforts cling to us. They may resurface at any time without warning. These may be unhealed traumas in our psyche that require the VA tool of trauma therapy. Certainly that is not the only source for rebalancing one's mind around sticky subjects, but we VAs have found trauma recovery to be paramount in continually improving our lives and the lives of our families, friends, and communities.

At times the VA may reach the sticking point. We say, "I have let go of many behaviors, but I will never give this up. The pleasure of this defect still outweighs the pain." Here we simply pray to be willing. Others might mutter to themselves, "OK, I'll head toward perfection, but I'm not in any hurry." We do not strive to achieve perfection. We leave that to the saints, who are far more qualified. We strive for progress rather than perfection. It is, however, not in our best interest to dally. As it states in AA's Twelve and Twelve, "Delay is dangerous and rebellion may be fatal. This is the exact point at which we abandon limited objectives and move toward God's will for us."

Step 7

Humbly asked God to remove our shortcomings.

This Step is the end of a self-centered life and the beginning of a life centered on God. If we are to overcome our more mild defects of character, we must first understand the meaning of humility.

Closely related to "humiliate," humility is often wrongly associated with negative feeling and meaning. While "humiliate" emphasizes shame and loss of self-respect, humility refers to humbling ourselves by relegating our reliance on pride. Humbling ourselves is the bedrock to this step and our recovery. Without humility, we are building our new house on a foundation of shortcomings. When we make the honest admission that we have created all we can on self-reliance, we VAs find ourselves capable of mustering the courage to see more clearly. Humility becomes the lens through which we can finally identify our unproductive ways for meeting our needs and what we think are the needs of others.

You may have heard the VA slogan, "It's not the WHAT, it's the WAY." This phrase holds true in most matters. The "WHAT" is fulfilling our needs. We all need what we need, and there is no shame in taking action to satisfy our needs. The "WAY" is how we go about satisfying our needs. We have gone about attempting to fulfill many of our needs by jumping on the Drama Triangle as persecutors, rescuers and victims. As persecutors, we demanded and threatened. As rescuers, we looked down our noses at those who refused our "help." As victims we have thrown tantrums, used depression and feigned helplessness. Each of these strategies have proven, at times, to be mildly successful but, if we are honest with ourselves, they have never satisfied our need for meaningful and lasting connection with others. Unconsciously, we have been relying on behaviors learned in the process of self-preservation and have mistaken them as healthy ways to meet our needs. For many VAs, these "self-preserving" strategies were born out of an experienced trauma. Each time we exercise the "unhealthy" strategy, we relive the trauma and build upon its hold over us. It is by understanding this phenomenon, and asking for God to remove it from us, that we VAs are enlightened to healthy strategies, which lead to true and lasting peace. For many of us Processing Triggers and neutralizing the trauma (anchor) under the trigger has become second nature. We have been practicing this since Step 2 and have found it paramount in turning our old way of thinking over to a power greater than violence. In Step 7 we reach for this tool again as our primary defense against our more subtle shortcomings.

Many of us have experienced abuse that society recognizes as illegal or immoral. Physical abuse, sexual abuse, financial manipulation, racism and sexism are simply the beginning of the list. Each of these traumas has affected the way we relate to people and society and ultimately the way we go about meeting our needs for certainty/comfort (safety, security), uncertainty/variety (new experiences), significance (feeling special), and connection/love. Many of us recalled our more glaring traumas, along with the traumas we inflicted upon others when we wrote down our history with violence in Step One and again in Step Four with our fearless and thorough moral inventory.

As an example of a subtler trauma, or what we VAs refer to as a "Chronic Trauma," let's consider having one's needs met inconsistently. Scientists have shown how inconsistent and random reward can create dependent behavior. In an experiment, scientists placed lab rats in a maze with cheese at the end. The rats eventually found the cheese and enjoyed a good meal. This could be translated as meeting the rat's need for security. The next day the cheese was not there. The rats, however, returned to the place the cheese had been. Randomly throughout the week the cheese was placed at the end of the maze. Whether the cheese was placed at the end of the maze or not, the rats were now expecting to find it in its regular place. They returned there daily regardless of whether the cheese was there or not. The scientists had created a pattern of inconsistent reward in the minds of the rats. One day the scientists decided to move the cheese to another location in the maze. Sadly, the rats had been conditioned by inconsistent reward to return to the same place long after the scientists had moved the cheese. Rather than finding the cheese in its new location, these rats continued to return to the original place despite starving themselves. By inconsistently meeting the rats' need for food, these scientists had programmed them to repeat a specific behavior, returning to the same place regardless of reward.

Another group of rats was placed in a different maze and given cheese in the same location everyday. One day, the scientists chose to no longer place the cheese in this location, but rather, to place it in another. The rats returned to the original placement of cheese only a few times before realizing that the cheese had been moved. They then worked to discover the new location and never returned to the original position.

We VAs have learned to empathize with ourselves and others trapped in a perpetual ride around the Drama Triangle because we all may have experienced this type of subtle but effective programming. Suppose a VA, whose default position on the Drama Triangle was Perpetrator, was able to meet their need for certainty, uncertainty, significance, and connection by shouting and "banging their high chair." This VA might intimidate people in an attempt to meet their own needs. Maybe every once in a while they were given what they demanded and felt that false power. Maybe other times they were reprimanded or punished, thus meeting their need for uncertainty and connection in a negative way. It's easy to see how this VA would continue this behavior well into adulthood until they were conscious of the damage it was causing themselves, their family, and their community. Isn't this VA just like the lab rat who returned to the same place looking for the cheese long after it had been removed? We have found that we no longer fear this person, but rather empathize with them, because we know that we too have behaved in this fashion. Like the lab rats, we have been mesmerized by inconsistent reward. If anyone understands the destructiveness of this behavior, it is us.

Consider the "Rescuer" who meets their needs for significance and connection by making themself out to be the "doormat." Perhaps, at one time in their life they were so scared about their own survival or wanting to feel important, that they developed the habit of carrying the emotional burden of a parent who was depressed or raged. This child grew into a person who might believe that they are only of value in a relationship if they forgo their own needs in order to help the "Victim." They take on the emotional weight of the other person and rescue them by doing for them what they, supposedly, can't do for themselves. Sometimes the child is given a warm smile or a "thank you." Other times, they receive a whine, a moan, a cold shoulder or a high volume complaint. Any of these responses deepens their resolve to rescue, since they are motivated by the unconscious belief that "if I just do it differently or better, I will get the love I need." Or "If I can put them at ease, I will meet my need for emotional safety (certainty) in this relationship." This child grows into an adult who through inconsistent reward has developed a lasting disposition toward rescuing behavior. VAs understand this very well. Most of us, if we are honest, have done, and continue to do, the same thing in more subtle ways than we could see when writing our Step One.

How about the VA who acts out the "Victim Role" more often than they are aware? Perhaps this person wants to say something positive, but can't stop themselves from saying something biting or inconsiderate. They might find it easier to shame someone into changing, than to admit their own feelings and needs. This person may have learned early in life that being rude was a way of meeting their need for connection, certainty and variety. Interrupting and not using "please" or "thank you," could have proven successful in getting not only attention (need for significance), but sometimes an adult might just give them what they want to stop them from whining or complaining. Perhaps this person didn't learn this behavior from lazy parents but from others, later in life, who shared the same ignorance of grace. This VA moans and whines their way throughout life often getting what they want. We VAs no longer feel frustrated by this behavior. We no longer rescue this person, by giving anything when they whine, nor do we allow them to annoy us to the point of retaliation with a sharp comment or, worse, a physically violent outburst. Those of us who thoroughly work Step 7 see this person in our own behavior and recognize it as a weakness that God can remove if we humbly ask. Even if we can't fully accept this victim's behavior we can empathize, using Nonviolent Communication, or pray for them rather than join them on the Drama Triangle.

So now we must summon more than the courage to admit that we are powerless over violence, as we did in Step 1. At this stage, we have a good understanding of how to abstain from violent behavior when it comes to the more glaring aspects of our disease. But what about the subtle nuances we uncovered in Step 6? Are we willing to let each of these go and re-create ourselves based on the will of God? Can we consistently and continually humble ourselves to God and not only ask for guidance, but listen to the response and follow God's lead? We now express enough humility to remain off of the Drama Triangle. Surely we can show enough humility to become truly happy.

When it comes to being people of high moral character, we have only begun to understand what that might mean. We understand that our thoughts lead to feelings, our feelings influence our actions, our actions form our habits and our habits become our character. We VAs have the habit of choosing violence as a way of meeting our needs, plain and simple. When violence worked for us, we redoubled our efforts. When it fell short we made ourselves out to be "the victim" of some person, place, or thing. When we failed to meet our needs in healthy, cooperative ways, thoughts of pride, greed, envy, anger, or lust took over, enhancing a belief that if we took more poison it would somehow nourish us. But that fantasy was always lacking in real substance. We tried sloth, gluttony, or depression, making ourselves out to be victims who the world had left behind. Unconsciously, we saw ourselves as someone who needed to be rescued. The shame of this pattern of thinking took us to new lows in self-esteem. Regardless of how we did it, our habit has been to operate from some position on the Drama Triangle. Surely by now we have a glimpse of the impact this habit has on our character.

Many of us understood that good character was desirable. But when we were confronted with character vs. comfort, our character was left behind in the pursuit of the comfort we imagined would make us happy. In many of our experiences we were carrying out the bad habits of generations before us. One thing is certain: any VA who is brave enough to travel through the door of humility found in Step 7 is a person who is willing to confront the idea that this cycle of violence began long before we were born and has been passed along through the ages.

I was determined that this cycle of violent behavior from generations before would stop with me. (One day at a time.) That my children would not have to suffer the separation from self that I, and many of my ancestors, suffered. Not because any of us were bad people, but because we had no understanding of the disease of violence. It is clear to any VA who has reached this milestone of embracing humility, that knowledge of this cycle alone is meaningless, without furthering our spiritual progress.

Now we ask ourselves to let go of what we may consider the milder malfunctions of our character. Those that may not immediately challenge our recovery, but that slowly and gradually erode our spiritual connection with life and ultimately compromise our chance for lasting happiness.

Every VA has felt the crushing blow of defeat. How else would we have been able to embrace our powerlessness over violence in Step 1? Some of us were driven to the rock bottom of death and prison before our eyes were opened to the possibility of a life without violence. To embrace some kind of humility was our only solace. It was by the humiliation of failure after failure that we became ready to embrace enough humility to admit that a power greater than ourselves could restore us to sanity. This path has not been easy. No VA has reached Step 7 without experiencing the pain of switching from self-reliance to reliance upon God, as we understand God.

Now we stand on the precipice of an entirely new frontier. We begin to see the benefit of seeking humility as a way of life. We embrace that working for humility is a life to be desired. Seeking and doing God's will has become our path away from violence and toward a life of meaning and contribution to our friends, families, and society. However, the desire to rebel can be even stronger. We have found that each stride we make into humility is met by a "test" of our faith. As if the universe conspires to support our new commitment to humility. "Are you sure you want to live a God-centered life?" It asks. Here, the opportunity to retreat back into violence presents itself, to test our newfound confidence in God's will. If we are in tune with our intuitive voice, we will find that we are no longer directed by the fears and guilt which once dominated our behavior. Instead, we are led to follow the more subtle voice of God in our lives. We humbly ask God to remove our shortcomings.

One of our major shortcomings is that we do not understand how to go about meeting our own needs in healthy ways. On this subject we may, at times, confuse our newfound humility with humiliation. The shame and embarrassment we feel is a one-way ticket back onto the Drama Triangle. Here we must turn over this shame to a higher power. There are as many ways to do this, as there are VAs. We all agree on one thing, a spiritual malady requires a spiritual solution. Here is the list of tools we use in "humbly asking God to remove our shortcomings." For the definitions of each tool refer back to Step 3 or visit www.violenceanonymous.org

---

Tools of Violence Anonymous

1. Sponsorship
2. Meetings
3. Literature/Readings
4. Service
5. Prayer/Meditation
6. Nonviolent Communication
7. Phone calls
8. Awareness
9. Processing Triggers (getting off the Drama Triangle)
10. Fun, Humor, and Laughter
11. Deep Breathing
12. Choice
13. Self-Care
   - Balanced rest
   - Balanced nutrition
   - Balanced exercise
14. Experience the feeling (sit with the feeling rather than

---

act on it)

15. Change Attention

16. Change Location

17. Safety Plan

18. Creativity

By applying these tools and others, we begin to feel the value of a nonviolent life, centered on God. Even those of us who had no faith in a power greater than ourselves awaken to the value of keeping a spiritual connection at the forefront of our lives. Those who thought themselves to be spiritual were amazed to find that they had been constrained by their own thinking. Step 7 is the beginning of our shift from a self-centered life toward a life guided by humility and service to God. As we begin to learn to meet our needs in healthy ways we better understand others and feel more connected to ourselves, our neighbors and to the God of our understanding. We become comfortable with the idea that we need not rely on pain to guide toward humility. We can begin to humbly reach for healthy alternatives to meeting our needs, out of habit, because we understand the pleasure of doing so. We VAs have found that in our pursuit of a happier life, the practice of this Step is fundamental to our goal.

"God I pray that my thoughts turn to gratitude and my actions are an example of your love. Thank you for guiding me to do your will."

Step 8

Made a list of persons we had harmed, and became willing to make amends to them all.

As it states in AA's 8th Step, "Steps eight and nine are concerned with personal relations." We must look back to survey where we have been at fault, make a vigorous attempt to repair the damage of our behavior and then clear the path for a new way of thinking that will become the foundation for peace and tranquility in our lives. With this state of mind we will mend and improve our relationships with others.

The idea of living in harmony with all people will be no small accomplishment. It is a path that we will constantly explore and strive to further. We have begun by admitting our powerlessness over violence and violent behavior, in Step One. In Step Two we make a start at coming to believe that a power greater than violence, has given us the grace to meet our own needs and support those we love in meeting their needs. In Step Three, we put that faith into action by consciously turning our will and our lives over the god of our understanding. The power we have found in VA guided us to meet our needs in cooperative ways that no longer compromise our integrity or the needs of others. In Steps Four and Five, we uprooted many of our trauma-based thinking patterns, resentments, fears, and sexual conduct and courageously battled forward by admitting the exact nature of our wrongs, to God and another human being. Steps Six and Seven gave us new tools for dealing with the more subtle forms of violent behavior and showed us that we could indeed become humble in the face of our higher power. Here we learned again to ask for help in honing our skills to remain free from the Drama Triangle. Now in Step

Eight we are asked to deepen our understanding of our Step 4 inventory and to, even more thoroughly, take responsibility for the wreckage of our past. Here we must again open old wounds and feel the shame and embarrassment of the situations that we attracted, through our addiction to drama. Those of us who have thoroughly worked Steps 1-7 understand with confidence that every interaction between human beings requires two or more people. This understanding gives validation to our belief that we may not be entirely to blame for the dynamic that has resulted in power struggles with others. We are, however, 100% responsible for the way we think and respond to these events and people. We may even understand, if only conceptually, that we have no real power to control anyone's behavior but our own. So it is fitting that here, in Step 8, we begin to recognize how we must own our part in each and every situation of discord, in order to carry on with a life of recovery from violence. We must begin to deepen our understanding that even our resentments and hurts are subtle openings onto the Drama Triangle. Every grudge we hold is a victim's mirage of false power. Every trauma that we refuse to heal is an opportunity to slide back onto the Drama Triangle; to create more pain and shame and weaken our financial prosperity. It is with this knowledge that we begin to embrace the benefit of cleaning our side of the street and the liberation that comes with making amends for the wreckage of our past.

Step Eight's purpose is to make a list of those we have harmed and prepare ourselves to right the wrongs we have done to others. What do we mean by "harm"? We could begin by examining how we have caused physical, emotional, mental, or spiritual damage. Did we exhibit the short fuse of the persecutor, employing our anger to force others to meet our needs at their expense? Did this behavior invoke fear, anger, or rebellion? Did we employ the rescuer's tactics of lying, cheating or seducing to trick a victim into relying on us? Or did we use the same tactics as a victim to fool others into meeting our needs instead of meeting them for ourselves? Did we play the victim to ensnare a rescuer who would care for us either financially, emotionally, physically or spiritually? This is not a complete list of the way we manipulated others to meet our needs. Let us look at some more subtle examples.

Perhaps we walked the earth unconscious that we were mildly triggered, thus making negative remarks or casting doubt on others' excitement. Perhaps we were irritable or cold due to our bad habit of triggering onto the Drama Triangle. What about wallowing in depression and self-pity? This self-abusive victim mindset can prove highly provocative to those around us. Especially when these persons are prone to rescuing or persecuting. The perpetually depressed person becomes an easy entry point and consistent invitation onto the Drama Triangle and, to the most disciplined mind, becomes a person to avoid. These behaviors are as equally damaging in the workplace as they are at home.

For many of us our first obstacle is the revelation that, since we are asking forgiveness from those we had harmed, perhaps we ought to consider forgiving those who have caused us harm. We may begin to realize that many of those we have been in conflict with suffer from the same malady as we. Since we now know how to give ourselves empathy for our needs and feelings, perhaps we can begin to use these skills regarding others.

There are also those instances where our behavior aggravated others to the point of triggering onto the Drama Triangle with us. Can we really hold onto blaming them for not being strong enough to resist our insistent invitation to join us in our wallowing? Let us keep in mind that we violence addicts often infuriate others with our unconscious need to play the victim or the rescuer. Only those well-trained in the art of remaining centered can remotely hope to resist the victim's invitation to persecute or rescue them. So let us cease to psychically rescue another by resenting their behavior, holding a grudge or even arguing with them in our heads. Let us, instead, muster the courage to focus on our need to feel at peace and increase our integrity. If we are truthful with ourselves we may recognize that, in many instances, we are dealing with people whose woes we have increased by our own lack of discipline. If we are considering asking for forgiveness, can't we also consider forgiving those whose actions we deemed harmful to us?

During this process of re-opening Pandora's box, some of us will feel such strong feelings of shame, guilt or sadness that we begin to deflect. Rather than sitting with the feeling, we will begin to focus on our victimhood, seeing only how they hurt us. Old habits can easily return, creating another test of our commitment to abstain from violent behavior (i.e., triggering onto the Drama Triangle).

When listing the people we have harmed, most of us became fearful when we realized we would be meeting face-to-face with them. We rescuers feared failing to meet our need to look good and be liked by others. We victims lacked confidence in our ability to refrain from falling into self-pity. We persecutors wondered if we had the discipline to resist the temptation to see ourselves as victims long enough to help meet the other person's need for safety. The thought of seeing, calling, or even writing people we had harmed became overwhelming. How could we possibly face the shame, embarrassment, and guilt of our past? We found comfort when our sponsors reminded us that, in Step 8, we are simply making a "list" of the persons we had harmed and becoming willing to make amends.

What about those who are happily unaware of the harms we caused them? Isn't it easier to leave them in the dark? Why must we even include them on our list? Will we let fear mixed with pride prevent us from making a list of all those we have harmed?

Some of us claim to have hurt no one but ourselves. Maybe we think our violent behavior was hidden away. Our depression didn't affect others. No one else had to endure the harsh judgments we piled upon ourselves. These were reserved for us alone. Perhaps we think that our home life didn't suffer because we always paid the bills. Or our business associates couldn't have been affected, since we always did our job. Our reputations were fine because few knew of our dramatic behavior. Those who did know took our side and saw us as the "innocent victim." What harm had we really caused, that a few simple apologies couldn't repair? This of course is the attitude of a fearful mind. And what VA can say, "I have never felt fear"?

With a clear focus on our need to heal and live without drama, we mustered the courage to accept that our behavior, whether as a victim, rescuer, or persecutor, affected most people we came in contact with, especially those closest to us. In Step 7 we realized that there is no shame in a person taking action to meet their own needs for certainty, comfort, variety, significance, connection, growth or contribution. However, we VAs, if we are honest with ourselves, have employed "ways" of meeting those needs that have caused pain and loss for others and have even prevented them from meeting their needs in cooperation with ours.

Having thoroughly worked Steps 1 through 7, we VAs have gathered a good deal of knowledge about violent behavior. We have a clear understanding of what thoughts can create roadblocks for us and what situations can prove treacherous in living a non-violent life. Perhaps we would like to make amends to certain people who are still heavily involved in violence. It may be too dangerous to make contact with these people. If we are savvy VAs, we now recognize a situation or person who would willingly damage our reputations, families, finances or well being. In these cases, our sponsor may suggest putting these people on a "maybe" or a "later" list on our 8th Step. At the very least, this amend could be made by a routine of honest and sincere prayer for that person's happiness. The same sponsor will remind us of the importance of putting those names somewhere on our list. At this stage of our recovery, we must decide each day to be honest with ourselves about our past. We must not hide from others and cannot hide from

God, as we understand God, if we expect to remain abstinent from violent behavior. Even though we might see wisdom in deferring action or in some cases can no longer make restitution to a person we have harmed, this should not deter us from making a complete and thorough list of our past life and how it affected others.

We may find that the harm we have done ourselves has been substantial. Emotional conflicts still persist in our unconscious. Some traumas have created violent emotional twists in our psyche that have colored our personalities and have redirected our thinking for the worse. Often deep, sometimes forgotten, trauma has taken root in our minds and bodies. In addition to these initial traumas, we have developed behaviors that continue to re-traumatize ourselves because of the "way" we have gone about meeting our basic needs. For most of us, the damage of shame, guilt, and embarrassment have dictated our behavior in ways beyond our conscious comprehension. Many of us began to understand in Step 7, that shame is a feeling generated from thoughts of inadequacy stemming from some past trauma. We understand that the best defense for feelings of shame is a consistent practice of neutralizing trauma and attending VA meetings. Here, our sponsor may direct us toward listing those areas where we feel shame on our 8th Step so that we can address them in our amends to ourselves, noting that we often feel shame as the result of having been traumatized by someone's behavior and have since carried their shame by unknowingly rescuing, persecuting or playing the victim. We may also be plagued by guilt, a feeling often derived from the thought that we have crossed our own moral line of conduct. Here we may want to make a list of these "guilt" situations so that we can begin to construct healthier ways of meeting our needs in situations like these in the future. The pain of embarrassment has often driven us to act out using different forms of power and control. Our sponsor will also encourage us to make a list of situations where we have used our embarrassment to justify triggering onto the Drama

Triangle. This will help us to develop more awareness around when we feel embarrassed. Even the simple awareness of the feeling can allow us to redirect our thinking and turn our focus toward clarity of our needs and requesting help in ways that create affinity and intimacy with others, rather than pain and frustration. For many of us, using the tool of Non-violent communication has become the path of amends to ourselves and others in situations where we used to be overwhelmed by feelings of shame, guilt and embarrassment.

Some VAs have questioned, "How can I make restitution without confidence that I have changed once and for all?" Here we must examine all our human relations. Should we VAs truly want to make amends to ourselves and others, we must reflect deeply on the thoughts that motivate our actions. We must become crystal clear about our needs and non-violent ways to go about meeting those needs. We must heighten our awareness of the tools of VA and allow ourselves to use them consistently and consciously. Once we have repeatedly practiced dealing with potential conflict in non-violent ways, we can rest in confidence that our amends are not hollow promises of change, but are in fact commitments to love and honor that, through our daily actions of non-violence, will lead to deep and fulfilling connections with family, friends, colleagues and new acquaintances. We develop a sense of knowing that, one day at a time, we are capable of backing our word with consistent acts of empathy, cooperation and kindness. We VAs who have crossed this threshold see this as the end of isolation and the beginning of connection with ourselves, others, and God.

Step 9

Made direct amends to such people wherever possible, except when to do so would injure them or others.

"Good judgment, a careful sense of timing, courage and prudence – these are the qualities we shall need when we take Step 9." Bill Wilson, founder of AA

After working Steps 1-8, many of us are confident that our habits are continuing to change. We may have even proven to ourselves that we can back-up an apology with consistently improving behavior. If so, we are ready to make restitution for the harms we have caused.

Once we have a solid understanding of those we have harmed and how we have harmed them, and have developed the correct attitude toward clearing our side of the street, we will want to determine the best course of action toward making amends.

With the guidance of our sponsors, we may want to group our amends into several classes. Those we will make right away. Those where only partial restitution can be made, since complete disclosure would cause more harm than good. Those where action should be deferred, and those where no direct amends or personal contact should be made at all.

We started the 9th Step process the day we admitted that we are powerless over violence. At this stage many of us wanted to shout from the rooftops that we had found a solution to the pain and suffering we had caused others and ourselves. Here, it was appropriate for us to acknowledge the harm our behavior had caused to our families and close associates, in a general way. Good judgment has taught us that, in the early days of recovery, it was best to avoid rehashing the details of our behavior. We have learned that taking our time to work Steps 1-8 has proven to be the best course of action toward making lasting and meaningful amends in Step 9. Enthusiasm alone cannot ensure that we have truly changed. Our Step 9 amends are of a different nature than the apologies made after the triggers, fights or violent outbursts of our past. While we are willing to admit the very worst, we want to avoid dumping our shame on someone else, by making amends too soon. Experience has shown us, the kindest course of action means holding our tongue until we have received solid and sound advice through prayer and council, and have had time to feel the changes of Steps 1-8 in our lives.

By exercising patience, we ensure that a consistent and lasting change can occur in our thinking, actions and character. This change is a natural extension of having honestly worked Steps 1 through 8. By this point in our recovery many of us have avoided and prevented enough potentially violent situations that we have begun to feel confident in our newfound behavior. This gives us the knowledge and belief that we have actually changed for the better, and with continued and consistent action we can increase our wellbeing and happiness. Our experience shows that, if we continue to work for it, we can rebuild the trust that we squandered through violence. One-day-at-a-time we can make amends resting confident with the knowledge that we have the tools to avoid repeating our past mistakes. As soon as we have proved to ourselves that we have indeed changed for the better, our confidence will be apparent to others. At this point in our recovery it is usually safe to speak honestly about our behavior with the people who have been adversely affected, even those who may have been only slightly inconvenienced, or are unaware of the harm caused.

It is at this stage that we can admit our wrongs, hear how our behavior has affected others, and make restitution without defensiveness or overwhelming guilt. Now we can go to those we have harmed, tell them about VA and explain what we are doing with our lives and our recovery. With this as the foundation for our discussion, we can admit our wrongs and make restitution. We can pay or make arrangements to pay our debts and financial commitments.

Sometimes we are surprised by the generous response of those we humbly face. Often our harshest critics will meet us halfway. There are those who will not be pleased to hear our amends or to even see us. It is their right to behave as they wish, but if we are prepared in advance for the worst case scenario, we will find that people on the Drama Triangle won't pull us back into violent thinking and defensiveness. We now have experience with using the tools of VA to help us deal with tricky situations. Others may play the victim and pray upon our weak nature, as rescuers, to take more than our share of responsibility. Here we summon all of our strength and knowledge of violent behavior. Since we are prepared for drama from people without VA knowledge, we can easily own our part, use Nonviolent Communication to mirror back what we hear them saying, and turn a potentially tense situation into one of mutual respect and understanding. In the worst cases we can do our best, wish them well and move on to our next amend.

The feelings of exhilaration, from the approval and relief of having made amends may make us hungry for more of the same. Some of us will feel so relieved that we are tempted to stop here rather than complete the rest of our list. We may be tempted to skip the worst or more embarrassing amends. On the other hand, a cold reception from others can spin us into a different type of fear. Let us be careful not to make excuses or procrastinate. These are signals that we are slipping into victimhood. We VAs understand where victim thinking can lead us.

Some amends will be postponed for legitimate reasons. Perhaps we need to raise the money to pay back an obligation. Since much of our manipulating behavior dealt with money, we find it best to consider financial violence as seriously as any other form of violent behavior. In some cases, our sponsors may advise to settle a debt rather than pay in full. However, where manipulation or coercion were involved, our sponsors will unanimously agree that paying in full is vital to our recovery.

Some amends might begin casually. Here we may use humor when describing how unmanageable our behavior had become, so as not to rehash old pains unnecessarily. This also helps us avoid any melodrama or playing the victim and seeking a rescuer. We are not looking for pity. We are here to demonstrate that we are becoming constructive members of our communities. We are capable of understanding the needs of others and are willing to help them meet those needs. No longer are we obsessed with ourselves or ashamed of how horribly we behaved.

In other situations a complete list of our abusive behavior is necessary to right our wrongs. Experience has shown that amends to intimate loved ones are best made with gentle care. We will want to prepare ourselves to listen to the other's account of our behavior with an open heart. Our willingness to own our part may require feeling deep embarrassment for past behavior. If this is the case, admitting these feelings aloud can be healing for the other party.

Sometimes we find that our shame is too great to make direct amends. Here our sponsors might suggest some trauma work on that specific issue (person, place or thing). After a thorough clearing of the trauma associated with this experience, and others like it, we can address this amend from a neutral state of mind.

There are cases where complete disclosure would cause harm to ourselves or others. Since we are dealing with an addiction to violence (violent thinking, people, and situations), we also understand those times when making direct amends would be dangerous. We VAs know from experience that living an open life without secrets is the most fulfilling and rewarding life. This is the life we seek and find on a daily basis. We also understand that there are times when complete disclosure could cause unnecessary suffering to innocent children, families, or businesses. Since we are dealing with violence, VAs also understand that exposing certain people with our full confession could lead to severe harm and even death. We may find it wiser and more savvy to find safer ways to make amends. In these cases, our sponsors may suggest that a commitment to changing our behavior and making amends in some way other than disclosure may be the best course of action.

Let's draw a clear distinction between amends that could result in embarrassment or financial loss, from our own unscrupulous desire to get what we wanted, and those where owning up could cause harm to ourselves or others. Experience has shown that overcoming fear of embarrassment or fear of losing what we have is imperative for long-term sobriety, peace-of-mind and happiness. An honest appraisal of each situation with our sponsors will reveal our true motivation for making or choosing not to make direct amends. Fear is not the correct reason to avoid making direct amends. However, if the other party has a propensity to take our admission, twist it and respond with violence toward us or others, we will want to find another way to make amends for our behavior.

Because our particular illness is one that creates violence, the savvy recovering VA acknowledges that we also attracted violent people into our families, businesses, and communities. Therefore, it is wise to acknowledge that some people we have harmed could use our honest admission to harm us emotionally, psychologically, physically or financially. VA experience directs us to use caution in making some amends directly. Perhaps our sponsor will tell us to prepare ourselves and wait for a safer point in time. They may also suggest that this amend may not be safe to make at all. In this instance, well-meaning VAs may choose to pray for this person instead of making a direct amend. If returning or paying back money might put people in physical danger, we may return it anonymously or find a charity as a beneficiary. If time and care are what we withheld, we might give that to someone else in need, to amend our behavior.

Let us keep in mind that each restitution requires a "living amend;" a continued commitment to behave differently when presented with similar circumstances. If our honest admission would harm an innocent person, our sponsor may suggest that we invoke a "living amend." Each day we commit to improving our character by changing our thoughts and actions, in the interest of striving toward spiritual living. They key is that we do everything in our power to clean our side of the street and live kinder lives.

During our practice of Step 9, we begin to see the Promises of VA revealing themselves in our daily lives. If we work for it, we find:

1. *Fear of conflict is leaving us. We understand how to engage others without drama.*

2. *We are developing the ability to meet our own needs while cooperating with others.*

3. *We no longer seek the approval of others as the measure of our worth.*

4. *We are not severe, nor do we coerce.*

5. *We leave others in absolute freedom of choice.*

6. *We are authentic and no longer pretend to be someone we are not, in hopes that others will meet our needs.*

7. *We are no longer hasty.*

8. *We find no pleasure in judgment.*

9. *We are attuned to our needs and the needs of others, regardless of the situation.*

10. *We understand others' needs, regardless of their communication style.*

11. *We are finding freedom from the power of guilt and shame.*

12. *Solutions that used to baffle us are now clear and often easier than we had realized.*

13. *We no longer regret or ignore our past.*

14. *We know peace.*

15. *We have a clear understanding of how our experience can benefit others.*

In practicing this step, our aim is to overcome our fear. The heart of Step Nine lives in our willingness to take full responsibility for our actions and show consideration for the well-being of others. To that end, we VAs sincerely move forward on the road of recovery from violent behavior.

Step 10

Continued to take personal inventory and when we were wrong, promptly admitted it.

In Step 10 we put our VA approach to the test. Here we determine if we can remain abstinent from playing the role of rescuer, persecutor or victim on a daily basis, under any condition.

Taking stock in our lives can happen for many reasons. Wise people make a common practice of looking for problems and finding ways to correct what is wrong. Doing so enables us to reconcile the past and meet the challenges of tomorrow as they come.

There are many ways to review the inner workings of our thoughts and actions in relation to our recovery from violent behavior. The first might be a spot-check inventory. Here we take a moment to "pause when agitated" and look at the possible source of our disturbance. We can do this whenever we need, throughout the day. The end-of-day inventory can serve as a balance sheet for the previous 24 hours. We give ourselves credit for our good deeds and accomplishments and debits for our failures, in the interest of learning from our victories and mistakes. Here we can work out plans of reward for successes and restitution for any harm caused that has not already been amended. We may also employ the time-frame inventory, where we take stock in a specific period of time, or since our last meeting with a trusted friend, sponsor or spiritual advisor. Many VAs practice annual or semi-annual inventories or take undisturbed retreats where we are able to reflect and meditate without the distractions of the outside world.

Some may ask, why spend all this time taking stock? Aren't there better uses of my time than constantly rewinding and re-hashing old problems? We VAs who have learned the practice of Step 10 understand the value of this time spent in review. We came to VA without a solid practice of appraisal regarding our dance with drama, and we found an opportunity in Step 10 to develop this skill. Continuous practice of this step will eventually prove so valuable that the time spent will seem inconsequential. This practice will eventually make the other hours of the day or year happier and more productive and can become a part of everyday living.

We VAs understand that, when we are disturbed it is the result of our thinking regarding some person, place, thing or situation. We cannot afford to waste the day on the Drama Triangle, making ourselves out to be a victim. These moments of dis-ease are appropriate times to practice a spot-check inventory. To identify our needs in the moment and the feelings associated with those needs. These spot-checks help us to begin to determine the difference between a strong emotion that triggers us into drama and one that triggers us into positive action and self-responsibility. Regular practice of Step 10 enables us to consistently meet our needs in cooperation with the other party.

We may run into unsettling surprises that take us off guard and set us off balance. In such tricky situations we practice neutrality; remaining off the Drama Triangle by using the tools of nonviolence. When triggers do occur we learn to employ self-restraint to minimize potential damage by holding our tongues or removing ourselves until we can regain composure and soundness of mind. By now we can all agree that when triggered, we are temporarily insane and in that state can do little to better a situation.

Now that we have some sobriety from violence we find that even though we have begun to regain the respect of our peers and family members, we must exercise extra care to ensure against taking too much credit for ourselves. There are times when great personal triumph has brought such joy, excitement and overwhelm that we celebrate with a step backward into violent thought or action. Are we blinded by self-importance and self-will, or are we simply frightened of this new found happiness and untrained in the art of graceful receiving? Has our newly found sense of security made it possible for us to confront even deeper and more unconscious fears and traumas? Here we must further our reliance on God. If we are honest in remembering how we came to VA and how we have grown under the care of our higher power, we can easily see how the true victory belongs to God.

As we grow in our recovery, it becomes easier to recognize when others are on the Drama Triangle and how to deal with that in a way that meets our need for safety, while exercising tolerance. We can admit, without shame, that we too have our moments of acting less than gracefully, and we can respond with empathy rather than judgment. This exercise of tolerance and empathy can lead to an understanding of true love for others. This transformation usually takes time. How many of us actually think and act with love and acceptance of everyone? Most of us love our close relations and friends deeply, show indifference to others, assuming they don't block us from our desires, and dislike or even hate the rest. By this point, most of us realize that we cannot go on thinking and relating to others in this fashion for much longer without a relapse. In Step 10 we learn to let go of this way of thinking entirely. The VA may exclaim, "But how do we exercise tolerance and empathy in all situations? We are not saints." Perfection will likely elude us. However, we have found from experience that if we suspend unreasonable demands, pray for those we dislike and show kindness to those who annoy us, we begin to develop grace. That grace is enhanced by the practice of Nonviolent Communication. Using NVC can guide us toward empathy for others in many circumstances that once rendered us powerless over violence.

Our daily inventory helps us to grow toward greater levels of grace by tracking our daily performance. How did we excel in listening to our own feelings and needs and balancing them with the feelings and needs of others? Did we empathize with others or argue? How have we acted in cooperation? Have we suffered because of our unwillingness to accept people, places and things? Did we promptly admit when we were wrong and apologize when necessary? When we develop this daily habit of self-examination, we find that thinking and acting with grace, kindness, courtesy and consideration becomes our modus operandi.

Each evening, perhaps before bed, many VAs tally up our daily inventory. We take stock of the pros and cons of our thoughts and actions for the day. How did we succeed without using power and control to meet our needs? Since many of us are predisposed to look at the negative, it is especially important for us to take into account our victories, large and small. This assessment of our kind deeds, good intentions, and empowering thoughts, can help us recognize their value and support us in continuing to improve. Even when we have failed, we can acknowledge our effort and learn from our mistakes. We remind ourselves that success comes from experience, and experience is often built from the lessons that accompany failure.

In admitting our failures, we may want to be honest about the motives behind our actions. Did we act out fear, anger, guilt, shame or self-centeredness? When we recognize our error, we can visualize how we would have preferred to behave and ask God's guidance in carrying that vision into tomorrow. We can follow up by making whatever amends may be necessary. It is critical that we avoid rationalizing our controlling behavior. Many of us have found a strong pull to fool ourselves, if we are even mildly triggered. Upon removing ourselves from the Drama Triangle and becoming neutral about a circumstance, we can see that our reaction may have contributed to disharmony. In these circumstances, amends are often required.

When we "taught someone a lesson," "constructively criticized," or "helped someone understand," we were likely rescuing or persecuting rather than truly helping the person. Our true motive may have been to make ourselves appear "powerful" at the expense of another or to change the other person so that we could feel safe. When we moaned and complained, we were playing the victim rather than contributing to the empowerment of ourselves and others. Learning to identify, admit and correct these mistakes is a building block to becoming increasingly conscious, enhancing our peace of mind and improving our character.

Honest atonement for harms done, gratitude for our blessings and a sincere effort to improve ourselves are the rewards of Step 10.

Step 11

Sought through prayer and meditation to improve our conscious contact with God, as we understood God, praying only for knowledge of God's will for us and the power to carry that out.

Prayer and meditation is our super highway to connecting with God, ourselves, and others. Like eagles soaring on an updraft, our souls ride the current of spiritual winds, tapping into a force that can carry us far further than our own flapping wings. Like the wind, it is a power that we can sometimes feel, yet cannot see. It is by utilizing prayer and meditation that we increase our awareness of this power and experience increased levels of consciousness.

In medical terms, even when behaving violently, we are considered conscious. We wake up in the morning and go about our day. But are we actually "awake" spiritually? Do we understand the true meaning of being conscious? Perhaps, that is something that we gradually understand in time. By now most of us have used prayer as a means of keeping our minds off of the Drama Triangle, but many of us still find the idea of praying and meditating a foreign one. Most of us are not interested in signing up for the life of a clergyman or priestess. Nor do we want to sit quietly bending our legs into pretzels while our backs ache. We simply want to remain free from drama and increase our level of wellbeing. Do we really need to seek a deeper connection with our creator in order to stay off of the Drama Triangle and away from violent thought or action?

VAs who identify themselves as Agnostics, Atheists, and sufferers of religious abuse may agree that the idea of prayer and meditation feels futile, at best. Why would we want to pray to a God who allows people to suffer, live in poverty, or die before their time? Some could argue that this is proof that there is no God at all. Still others would be right in fearing to follow anyone who claims to hear or know the voice of God. Haven't we endured enough trauma from the tongues of the religiously righteous? Didn't many of us find as much psychological violence in the church as we did in the street? How do we know we are not falling into a similar trap?

Others confessed that the existence of millions of suns, planets, and dark matter, must surely be evidence of something greater than us, but that doesn't mean we believe in the existence of a God that cares about human beings. By this point in our recovery, each of us has grown considerably in understanding and abstaining from violent behavior. Sure, we have grown to like and even trust VA, and we are grateful for the miracles we have witnessed in recovery from violence, but we are not enthusiastic about prayer and meditation. Our sponsors may encourage us here by pointing out that each step we have grudgingly taken has resulted in far more recovery than backsliding, and if we can find the courage to try something new we may find something unexpected.

Finally, we decided to experiment with prayer and meditation and found the result to prove useful. We felt more at ease, more capable and, with practice, began to know that a change for the better had come to pass. Regular practitioners of prayer and meditation can no more live without it than without air, water, or food, if they hope to continue their neutrality and peace of mind. Through our own experience we began to understand that we were nourishing our souls and developing a connection with our intuition. By bouncing these intuitive thoughts off of our sponsors and fellow VAs, we began to develop trust and confidence in ourselves once again. Exercising a quiet mind brings us to a more neutral place of being that allows us to listen to others with the same steady calm. These skills enable us to experience people, places and situations more neutrally. We can avoid taking sides or taking offense and choosing to play the role of victim. By attuning our senses, to more deeply connect with ourselves, our environment and our creator, we began to understand how to connect with others more deeply.

There is a power from the combination of self-evaluation, prayer, and meditation. Practiced separately, each has a strong impact on our health and wellbeing. Used in combination, they become an even stronger force in the foundation of our recovery from violence and illuminate our path to a fulfilling and happy life. With consistent practice, we VAs develop the ability to experience the presence of our Creator and to align our will with God.

In Step 4 and again in Step 10 we begin to understand how self-evaluation gives us humility and grace. By examining the darker currents of our nature we develop a strong understanding that we need God's love, support and help. This is the beginning of replacing arrogance and shame with humility and grace. It is through prayer and meditation, in Step 11, that we are empowered to take this understanding further. Now we begin to align our true selves with the will of the universe and its natural laws. We develop calm steady confidence that we can serve God, ourselves and others with each thought and action. Through prayer and meditation our need for contribution is awakened. Our confidence, that we have something of value to contribute, grows into the norm rather than the exception.

How do we meditate? Throughout the centuries men and women of faith have filled libraries, places of worship and now the Internet with volumes of information on meditation. Some

VAs have the benefit of a positive connection to a spiritual practice or religion that already includes meditation. We hope that you will return to that practice with renewed vigor. What about the rest of us who have no idea where to start? It was suggested in the very first 12 Step program to find a "really good prayer." You may have one in mind already. If not, try this prayer from Saint Francis of Assisi. Though you may not appreciate his religious position as a Catholic Priest, you might relate to his struggles as a person. After coming out of a painful experience, this prayer was born.

"Lord, make me an instrument of thy peace.

That where there is hatred, I may bring love;

That where there is wrong, I may bring the spirit of forgiveness;

That where there is discord, I may bring harmony;

That where there is error, I may bring truth;

That where there is doubt, I may bring faith;

That where there is despair, I may bring hope;

That where there are shadows, I may bring light;

That where there is sadness, I may bring joy.

Lord grant that I may seek rather to comfort than to be comforted;

To understand, than to be understood;

To love, than to be loved.

For it is by self-forgetting that one finds.

It is by forgiving, that one is forgiven.

It is by dying, that one awakens to eternal life. Amen."

Many of us find it useful to re-read this prayer and ponder on what each word means to us. We might take five deep breaths and search our minds for what it means to bring love, forgiveness, harmony, truth, faith, hope, light, and joy. We might simply clear our minds of all thoughts and feel the sensations in our body after reading such a deep and meaningful petition, focusing on the sounds in the room and the rhythm of our breath. Allowing ourselves to be lifted up and inspired. We will want to avoid any chatter or debate in our minds. Meditation is a time to observe. When we notice resistance, we redirect our attention back to our breathing or the question, "what does this prayer mean?"

My own experience with meditation is one of learning to focus my mind and my attention. To notice thoughts as they come up and to let them go as easily as they appear, trusting that I will retain what is necessary for the next step in my evolution. When I have a challenge, I simply ask for guidance on the issue and breathe until a solution comes to me, rather than using my un-assisted intellect to solve it. Since sitting and quieting my thoughts is difficult for me, I was relieved to learn that Kung Fu Masters would rigorously exercise before sitting to meditate. This practice allows stress to leave the body and endorphins to flood into the brain, creating a more positive environment for focused thinking. By exercising first, I find it much easier to meditate. I even consider my physical exercise a form of meditation since it calms my mind and allows me to perceive my life more clearly.

Some VAs may think this is nonsense and completely impractical. "If I spend my whole day sitting and breathing, how will I ever get anything done?" When we find ourselves here, it's helpful to remember how much time we spent arguing and fighting with others in our minds or face-to-face. How often did we take offense to someone's comments rather than asking for clarification of their meaning? How long did we wallow in self-pity or hold grudges in silence? How much of our precious lives did we spend trying to bend someone to our will, then complaining or acting out when they did not submit? Now that we are on the path to arresting that behavior and replacing it with more productive thoughts and actions, we can see how we have more than enough time to meditate. Think of this as drawing up your spiritual blueprint. In order to build anything that will last, we must first envision it and plan for it. This is what meditation does for our spiritual connection with life. It aligns us with what is real, but unseen. Sometimes, the voice of God comes in a whisper. By meditating, we quiet ourselves enough to hear it.

So back to the prayer we go with our meditation, questioning what it might mean to comfort, rather than to be comforted; to understand than to be understood; to love than to be loved. Whether we choose to use the examples here or others discovered by ourselves, we recognize that there are many paths to connect with our creator. With time and practice, we begin to experience grace, wisdom, love and compassion in our daily lives.

Here are just some of the practical benefits of meditation:

1. With the aid of advanced brain-scanning technology, researchers are beginning to show that meditation directly affects the function and structure of the brain, changing it in ways that appear to increase attention span, sharpen focus and improve memory.

2. The same research has shown that meditation increases the actual size of your brain.

3. Other research shows that people who meditate are physiologically younger than those who don't meditate.

4. Increased emotional balance.

5. Increase intuition and ability to act on intuition.

6. Reduced blood pressure and improved immune system function.

7. Reduced stress and anxiety.

How do we pray? The Oxford Dictionary defines prayer as a solemn request for help. Common understanding acknowledges a lifting of one's heart and mind to God. There are as many ways to pray as there are people willing to engage in the practice. Some prefer to ask God for blessings, others converse with God, bearing their deepest joys, fears and pains, and still others express their gratitude. Once we have made a start, we usually find a form of prayer that works for us as individuals. When in doubt, we might consider returning to the prayer of Saint Francis or another writing from the spiritual practice of our choice.

Those of us who are sincere about prayer may want to consider "the way" we pray. Are we on or off of the Drama Triangle? Are we praying as a victim or as someone truly mustering the courage to serve God and others? Certainly, if we do ask for God's favor, we want to ask for those things that we, and others, most need.

Consider the VA who, with good intentions, prays as a rescuer; diagnosing those around them and asking God to fix this or that about another's thoughts, behavior or character. In addition to adding the phrase, "if it be thy will, God," this VA might benefit from a close examination of what they need, and how they can ask for that need, using non-violent communication rather than coercion and manipulation. Their sponsor might suggest that this VA do some trauma work and limit their prayers for the other person, to those things they wish for themselves, such as happiness, health and prosperity.

How about the VA who prays as a persecutor; shouting at God to give them their way. This person might need to use the VA Tools to remove themself from the Drama Triangle before they can truly benefit from prayer. Perhaps a good course of trauma work will help them find a deeper connection to the God of their understanding and allow them to find peace and neutrality when asking for guidance. From each emotional challenge, we are turning the poison of pain into the medicine of a deeper understanding of oneself. When we understand our thoughts, feelings, and needs, we can channel that through prayer. This action deepens our commitment to a reliance on God as we understand God.

When we struggle to untangle our prayer life from violent thinking, we can fall back on the wording of Step 11 "…praying only for knowledge of God's will for us and the power to carry that out." So how does a VA recognize "knowledge of God's will"? If at a loss, we might return to the prayer of St. Francis or to our sponsors. We want to ensure that we are listening to our God-centered intuition, rather than a self-serving voice that would have us meet our needs at the expense of others.

In the morning we may turn our attention to the coming day, asking for guidance in our daily activities and work. As the day progresses we may want to return to prayer during difficult situations, asking for assistance in remaining neutral and off of the Drama Triangle. When we find ourselves in a mildly triggering situation, many fall back on the prayer, "God, I pray to find in you what I may be looking for in this person, place, thing or situation, and I pray that this person, place, thing or situation find in you, what they may be looking for in me." Some VAs like a regular routine of prayer, praying at the top of every hour, just to remind themselves of some blessing or gratitude. Others pray each time they visit the restroom, to ensure that they are remaining connected with the God of their understanding multiple times each day.

At day's end, most VAs return to prayer by expressing gratitude for successes and lessons learned. Before sleep, we may ask for assistance with any challenges encountered, while noting them in our Tenth Step inventory. The main point is that we do this without the belief of victimhood, but instead with the humility of a recovering VA who is learning to live neutrally and without drama.

It is through practicing Steps 1-10 that we begin to consistently meet our needs for certainty/comfort, uncertainty/variety, significance, connection/love and growth. Experience shows that, when these needs are consistently met, we VAs can easily focus on our 6th basic need; the need to contribute to the wellbeing of our families, communities and society as a whole. By practicing prayer and meditation in Step 11, we strengthen our ability to meet our need for contribution, by developing our ability to discern God's will and to carry it out. It is during the process of a daily practice of prayer and meditation that we begin to trust that we are becoming healthy and able to care for our needs and the needs of others without fear of causing damage. We begin to feel God's assurance that we are on the right path toward doing good works for ourselves, our loved ones and society as a whole.

This may be good news for the VA who feels cut off from a spiritual connection or who has yet to experience the power of prayer and meditation, due to trauma or differing belief. Many of us experienced religious trauma under guidance from those who used manipulation or power and control to shame us mentally, psychologically, and, in some cases, physically. These VAs often need extra support while re-engaging in prayer and meditation. Reaching for the guidance of a sponsor, fellow VAs and trauma work has proven crucial for many of us who have braved the path of reconnecting to our intuition. We have found the process to be enlightening and have developed a discipline that, when practiced off of the Drama Triangle, is rewarding and fulfilling. The unbeliever who continues to doubt the power of prayer and meditation will find through practice, however slight, that their state of mind becomes more positive. We begin to notice a profound decrease in the amount of time spent in "Victim" thinking and an increase in our ability to remain neutral and open to grace.

There are also times when we can't or won't bring ourselves to pray. Here we find it best to explore our unmet needs and find healthy ways to meet those needs, off of the Drama Triangle. These triggered moments of deep frustration and rebellion can be a beacon of light into an unhealed trauma that has been plaguing us for years. Once the trauma has been neutralized, we find it easier to return to a state of gratitude where prayer and meditation can be easily continued.

The rewards of prayer and meditation are only partially understood and are perhaps immeasurable. The fact remains, for we VAs who practice Step 11, that we experience a deeper sense of peace when seeking and acting on God's will for us. We no longer live in fear that we will lose ourselves in drama, but instead live in gratitude and grace. Our ability to recognize love, kindness and humility in our thoughts and actions is mirrored by the people, places and situations that we attract. Meeting our basic needs for certainty/comfort, uncertainty/variety, significance, connection/love and growth through cooperation become second nature. Our thoughts are far less clouded by "victim" thinking and are instead focused on our need to contribute to the wellbeing of others. Solutions that used to baffle us are now clear and often easier than we had realized. This comes from our commitment to creating space for the voice of intuition and a connection with God as we understand God.

Step 12

Having had a spiritual awakening as the result of these Steps, we tried to carry this message to others, and to practice these principles in all our affairs.

At this point in our recovery from violence, we realize that meeting our need for contribution toward others, our families, and our communities, can lead to a fulfilling life of joy and peace. It is through working the previous 11 Steps that we have cultivated a consciousness of our thoughts, feelings and actions. This level of consciousness, we refer to as a spiritual awakening.

There are likely to be as many definitions for a spiritual awakening as there are people who claim to have had one. Perhaps it is best for each of us to choose our own definition. We can all assuredly agree that each definition has in common a deeper sense of knowing, accepting and loving ourselves and others. Can we further agree that our accomplishments are far greater for having had an awakening, than they were with unaided will power? This can be supported by the recollection that our unaided will power brought us to a violent rock bottom, and a gradual awakening has led us out of that pit and into the light of day? Now we sense a deeper understanding of compassion and love. We understand how to behave in ways that express empathy and kindness. We see that our relationships are no longer doomed, but instead full of promise and opportunity. By working VA's first 11 Steps, we have contributed to this awakening and prepared for its appearance. One day at a time, we have tethered ourselves to an anchor that holds us firmly when storms challenge our newfound peace.

Now in Step 12, we engage in carrying the VA message into our practice of daily living. By continuing to work all 12 Steps we become living examples of the power of recovery, and we are able to help others freely and willingly. This is perhaps the most rewarding step in our recovery and our lives.

In Step 1 we admitted we were powerless over our violent thoughts and actions, and that our lives had become unmanageable. Here we felt the pain of our past. We acknowledged our failure to meet our needs without hurting others and ourselves. We examined what it meant to live on and off the Drama Triangle and the effects of living as a rescuer, persecutor, and victim. In Step 2 we began to understand the warning signals that lead to triggers and we began to glimpse how trauma and lack of discipline drive us onto the Drama Triangle. This is where we began to understand how deeply ingrained our unnatural violent habits had become. We became open to the idea that a power greater than violence could restore us to sanity. In Step 3, we turned our will and our lives over to that power, by utilizing the tools of VA. This practice taught us the discipline of interacting without using power and control to meet our needs. Through daily repetition of VA's tools, we began to rebuild faith in ourselves, find faith in a power greater than violence and meet our needs in cooperation with the needs of others.

Our searching and fearless moral inventory led us to understand how we repeatedly engage in patterns of violence and relive prior trauma while blaming others for our woes. In Step 4, we developed clarity of our needs and an understanding of how we had used violence in meeting those needs. Whether we had learned these methods from example or by our own creative resources, we understood the urgency in letting these habits go and replacing them with healthy ways to care for ourselves and others. We more deeply understood the value of trauma recovery and its importance for our continued health and happiness. We looked closely at how our addiction to violence damaged the lives of innocent bystanders and loved ones. We took our Step 4 inventories to our sponsors or trusted council in Step 5. Now we could finally let go of the guilt and shame we had carried for too long. By admitting to God, ourselves and another human being the exact nature of our wrongs, we found new freedom from the grips of isolation. We sensed a deeper level of honesty and connection with colleagues, friends and families.

In Step 6 we took a closer look at our so-called, defects of character and became ready to have them removed. At this stage, some of us hesitated. We were willing to let go of the more glaring flaws in our behavior, but these milder defects we enjoyed, and saw no reason to give up completely. We determined that even though we refused to let go today, we would cease to cry "never" and show the willingness to remain open and change. By examining our behavior more carefully, we found the more subtle ways in which we employed violence to meet our needs. We began to understand our low level triggers, which helped us to see more clearly that when we were feeling resentful, sad, angry, hurt, betrayed, anxious, depressed, guilty, etc., we were often playing the victim role on the Drama Triangle.

In this phase of our recovery we realized that the world was not out to harm us, as we had previously thought. We developed trust in ourselves to behave neutrally and lovingly. We began to differentiate between those we could trust and those we could not. We realized that despite having a history of trauma, not everyone in our lives meant us harm. In fact, many people we considered close to us were worthy of our trust. With our newfound respect for life, we began to shift our behavior in ways that helped others feel better about themselves while remaining true to our own needs. Simultaneously, we began to understand that no one person would successfully support us in every aspect of our lives. While taking a closer look at the positive and negative ways we met our needs and drilling down, to further understand the power of our own character defects, we were amazed to realize that a savvy VA can select different people to help them with different needs. In other words, we no longer called a plumber to fix the roof, just because we felt we owed him or liked his company. Instead, we learned to ask for help from those we were sure had the experience needed. We also resolved to give help only when it was requested of us. Listening and speaking using Non-violent communication became one of our most powerful tools.

Humbly asking for God's help in our quest to improve ourselves was our introduction into Step 7. Here we learned the difference between humiliation and humility. We put our focus on how we could contribute to the wellbeing of others rather than simply focusing on our own needs. We began to understand that it is not "what" we do, but the "way" we do it that determines how we impact the lives of those we commune with.

In Step 8, we made a list of the people we had harmed and became willing to make amends to them all, taking into account everyone we had rescued and persecuted. We began to recognize how we must own our part in each and every situation of discord, in order to carry on with a life of recovery from violence. Here we vowed to improve our discipline for remaining neutral by committing to no longer indulge in "victim thinking" and to clean our side of the street. Next we made direct amends to those we had harmed, except when to do so would injure ourselves or others. In doing this, we found a new confidence in this way of living and experienced the promises of VA coming true in our lives.

In Step 10 we developed the habit of daily self-examination and house cleaning. When we were wrong, we promptly admitted it. This practice put our newfound humility into action and helped us to choose empathy and tolerance over the Drama Triangle.

By this point, we understood that a power greater than violence had restored us to sanity. The practice of prayer and meditation led us to a deeper connection with that power in Step 11. Here we learned that taking the time to pray and meditate was paramount in increasing the distance between drama and our desired state of peace. When we applied ourselves to prayer and meditation, our access to intuition, grace, and patience, increased our connection with God as we understood God. By praying only for God's will and the power to carry that out, we began to reap the rewards of service.

Having worked these first 11 Steps, we rest confident in the fact that we have experienced a spiritual awakening. Here we are able to look at the newcomer, who is baffled by this spiritual angle, and know that with perseverance they may also know the God of their understanding and find freedom from violence. We understand that, with the application of these steps, those who are willing to change, find peace. In Step 12 we share what we know with other suffering violence addicts, and find this generosity to be the true payoff for Violence Anonymous. We agree that love is most strongly experienced when it is given. This is a natural law of living. Now, in Step 12, we feel the power of VA as we give to others what was freely given to us.

Even the newest of newcomers can experience the power of 12 Step work. This VA may feel beaten down and full of shame about their own situation, but they received unimaginable rewards by speaking in a meeting. This VA's honest account of their own burdens gives hope to others who had none and reminds the old-timer, full of faith, how their life once was. By sharing honestly with another violence addict, the newcomer brings healing to themselves and others.

How about the sponsor who guides another through the 12 Steps of VA? This person gives freely, without expectation of recompense. By divine paradox, this VA finds that giving is its own reward. Experienced VA's agree, by sharing the VA message one experiences an unmatched satisfaction. Looking back at our 4th Step inventory of needs, we find that service to other VA's meets our need for contribution and steers us toward a fulfilled life.

Practically all VAs enjoy the experience of a successful 12th Step. Some might even say the greatest satisfaction and most rewarding joy is giving back to the newcomer whose pain and misery is quenched by the knowledge and experience that we have found. Who doesn't revel by seeing a new light in eyes once dark? By hearing the tone of voice change in a newcomer who finally understands their part in drama? By helping a VA who carried so much shame find peace? By witnessing another sick and suffering violence addict grow and recover? We love to see individuals change the course of their lives, reunite their families and cooperate with kindness and empathy. Seeing the outcast welcomed back into the community or career path lifts our hearts. We are inspired by their newfound peace and behaviors that warrant trust and confidence rather than fear and anger. We enjoy seeing them cultivate grace from their relationship with God. These are the rewards of VA's 12th Step. All of these things are what we VAs have been given, and what we carry to the still sick and suffering violence addict.

We listen in meetings to receive and give assurance to fellow VAs who could not recover alone. When we speak, we do our best to carry the message of recovery. Whether we are speaking with one or many, we consider it 12th Step work. For those who prefer not to speak up in meetings there are many other ways to remain active in the 12th Step. Those who help provide coffee and snacks at face-to-face meetings can be VA's unsung heroes. Much comfort can be given to newcomers after meetings. Simple small talk, laughter, and companionship can prove a great relief to those new to recovery and can help the newcomer find common ground in VA. We recall that which was so generously given us and pay-it-forward to the still sick and suffering violence addict.

Since we have often sought to help others and ended up creating tension and discord, we fall upon the question, "How do we practice the 12th Step without rescuing?" Some of us may find it difficult to spend time sharing our experience with a prospective VA, who is not quite ready to give themselves the gift of freedom from drama. We may slip into self-pity or sadness to watch a newcomer backslide or leave VA. Here it is important to make a distinction between helping and rescuing. When we truly help someone, we care as much for their autonomy as we do for our need to contribute to their wellbeing. Should they choose to falter on the path to non-violence, we must employ the discipline to allow them to learn in their own way, in their own timeframe.

Perhaps we have great success in helping newcomers. So much so, that we are looked up to as an expert in recovery. Here we face a different challenge. We may become possessive of the newcomers, giving advice on matters we are not qualified to give. This type of rescuing can create confusion and eventual backlashes. We have found that sticking to our experience is the best way to assist others.

A well meaning VA can often confuse helping with rescuing, by giving unsolicited advice. We have found that assistance given prior to a request for help can sometimes cause more harm than good. Why waste good counsel on someone who is not ready to hear it? Isn't it best to wait for the newcomer to request guidance, before rushing in with unwanted council? This approach can be painful for a VA prone to rescuing, who can clearly see a solution for someone still active in violent thought and behavior. By this point in our recovery, we are savvy enough to know that rescuing someone will not only fail to help them, but could also result in a dance around the Drama Triangle and cause harm to ourselves. Here we practice the principle of attraction rather than promotion. Better to lead by example and allow another to ask for help before giving advice. This empowers us to avoid the habitual pull toward rescuing and brings us closer to meeting our need for contributing to the wellbeing of others. Rather than push our ideas on people, we have learned to ask a simple question, "Can

I make a suggestion based on my experience?" Perhaps we want to take things a step further and utilize Nonviolent Communication to simply mirror back a newcomer's feelings and needs. Sometimes the best 12 Step work is done with an expression of empathy.

Now we come upon the second half of VA's 12th Step: Practice these principles in all our affairs. Can we carry the example of VA into every aspect of our lives? Are we able to live with the spirit of love and tolerance? Can we bring the same level of faith and confidence to those we meet in daily life, as we do to newcomers in VA? How will we deal with success and failure? Will we allow our thoughts to trigger us onto the Drama Triangle, or will we accept the ups and downs of life while remaining neutral and focused on service to God and others? Will we succeed in bringing the spirit of VA into our work and home life? Can we deepen our devotion to the religion or spiritual practice of our choice? Can we bring a new level of joy with us along our path? Yes we can! The evidence is in our experience. We have seen VAs navigate some of life's more painful and joyful experiences by leaning on the 12 Steps, the tools and other VAs for guidance and support. We have drawn inspiration from those who have developed the ability to turn an abusive past into an example of happiness and healthy living.

Despite great victories, none of us have been able to exhibit perfection in our daily living. Take the VA who has a good deal of success in abstaining from violence by working some of the steps. They find new happiness in their family and work life. They begin to understand some of the VA Tools and concepts. They feel satisfied and decide there is no need to continue on with all 12 Steps. They are doing fine on only a few. They may begin to congratulate themselves prematurely or fall into indifference. This is what our AA friends refer to as "two-stepping," and it can go on for years. Even the brightest can fall for this illusion, but our success is short lived. Failure to continually work all 12 Steps soon results in the return of our old ways of thinking and acting. At this stage the VA might begin to feel discouraged and doubt the effectiveness of this simple program.

The VA might suddenly hit a rough patch and become filled with fear or frustration. That hoped-for job didn't come through. The lay-off or heartache of losing a loved one renders us powerless over "victim thinking." How can we practice VA's principles during the dark times? Here, we do our best to sit with the feelings rather than act on them. When thrown for a loop, we search ourselves for deeper trauma that may be binding us to the Drama Triangle. We might utilize the tools of trauma therapy, Reframing, EMDR, EFT or other means of untangling our thinking from historical pain. We find comfort in prayer, meditation, and helping the newcomer. In time, we find that what appeared to be poison can be transformed into medicine. In other words, if we are able to switch from "two-stepping" to "twelve-stepping ," our experience will one day benefit others in ways that fulfill our need for contribution to our families, friends and communities. In this way, we express our willingness to receive the grace of God and show evidence that weathering any storm is possible.

When we practice these principles in all our affairs, most VAs are able to handle what life throws our way. During adversity, we can take the difficulty in stride and create demonstrations of faith. Regarding finances, romance, and friendship, we have found that remaining free of the Drama Triangle is crucial to making and protecting all types of wealth. Regardless of whether we are up or down on fortune's wheel, we can turn our situation into an opportunity for growth and contribution. Spiritual development is the answer to all our woes. We rely on this simple program to guide us toward serving God.

The way we go about meeting our needs changes and grows as we develop spiritually. What was once a violent expression of a basic need (judging, manipulating, shouting to coerce others into helping us cope) has now become a neutral request full of empathy. Our needs are easily expressed without fear and our ability to listen for the needs of others has become paramount for living peacefully. We used to demand and dominate. Now we request and receive. We used to be over dependent on others, unconsciously looking for a rescuer. Now we depend on God and ourselves to meet our own needs. When others submitted to our domination we thought we were happy. When they began running away, standing up to us, or refusing our unsolicited advice, we suddenly saw ourselves as victims. We used shame and blame to force others into submission, rather than realizing our behavior was the problem. When we played the victim and insisted that others take care of our emotions and affairs (that the world owed us), the result was our own misery and disgust from those around us. Our behavior resulted in loss of friends, missed job opportunities, divided communities and weakened family ties.

The trauma from past violent experiences was keeping us frozen in violent behavior. We hoped that someone would rescue us. No one could. Parents, wives, husbands, friends, family, bosses: we drove them all away. Our over-dependence on others became our Achilles heel, though in most cases we could not see it or understand it. It was up to us to neutralize our original traumas, with the help of trusted friends and professionals, while working all Twelve Steps. By doing so, we set about changing our orientation toward "victim thinking" into a habit of self-responsibility and faith.

Spiritual progress has been the solution to all of this. At our rock-bottom, we saw clearly how destructive our behavior had become. Today we use the VA Tools and work the 12 Steps to bring our thinking around to sanity. We begin to meet our six basic needs in ways that express cooperation with the needs of others. By doing so, we have broken our isolation and found joy in communion with our fellows. No longer do we have to endure the loneliness of being overbearing or over-dependent. It was "victim thinking" that isolated us from connection with others. Through practicing these principles in all our affairs, we have found a way back to meaningful and fulfilling relationships. No longer do we live in fear that we will hurt others in the pursuit of our needs, and no longer do we take offense, when others rudely stumble toward needs of their own.

Many of us experience the desire to partner with another mentally, emotionally, physically, and spiritually. We may wish to seek a way to meet our need for love and connection through marriage or a committed relationship. Despite our desire to be loving and kind, many of us, through ignorance, self-will, compulsion, or otherwise, have managed to make a mess of it. Somehow, despite our best efforts, our attempts at drawing loved ones close to us only led to pushing them further away. In short, our endeavors to meet our need for healthy love and connection, led to unhealthy connection, frustration, loneliness and pain. With the practice of VA's 12 Steps, Tools, and meetings, we are beginning to experience the life full of loving connection and peace we have always sought. A life that is achieved through consistent works.

Let's take the newcomer, who has managed to hang onto their marriage despite their disease's best effort to snuff it out with violence. This VA unconsciously viewed themself as a victim for years. They either wallowed in self-pity or acted out physically to meet their needs for connection and significance, pouting and shouting their way into feeling important. Their partner took on the role of rescuer, scurrying around them, walking on eggshells, working to please at the expense of their own needs. This partner may have become the primary breadwinner, mother or father figure, or the emotional doormat, to create what they thought was a peaceful home, but in the end they failed to save the violence addict from their own disease. Now the addict has found VA and is beginning to get the drift of this spiritual program. They are finding strength in recovery and even managing to remain free from the Drama Triangle for good stretches of time. They are noticing a shift in their partner's behavior. The partner has moved from living life as a Rescuer to seeing themselves as a Victim to the years of heartache and disappointment. After all, they have been playing the role of the "responsible one" and have bypassed their own needs for the needs of the Victim and/or bully.

The partner may begin to act out the Persecutor role by picking fights or creating traps for the VA to step into. This is the first real test of this VA's recovery. Can they utilize what they have learned in VA to remain neutral while their partner goes through this phase of letting go of the shame and resentment they have carried for years? The partner may be experiencing deep sorrow that all their years of rescuing have failed to change the addict, and now VA has begun to do what they could not. The partner may also begin to wonder if they can trust the VA to take care of themselves and the family, unconsciously testing them to see if they will relapse into old behavior or prove to be an honorable and gentle partner. They may also be struggling with understanding that, in a relationship, it is not reasonable to think that one person can be the "violent one" and the other person be perfect. They may be coming to terms with the idea that they have been committed to a violent relationship due to their own traumas and habits. This revelation may be hitting them rather hard.

At this stage, seeing their unhappiness, the VA may be tempted to play the Rescuer and give unsolicited advice. After all, this newcomer has found a solution to their violent behavior and can see that their partner may benefit from what they have found in the 12 Steps of VA. Here the VA member should pause and reconsider. Experience has shown us that until the partner asks for help, advice is not only useless, but will undoubtedly be considered an affront. Rescuing is an act of violence. The VA member will be far more successful using empathy.

During this time, the partner's opinion may be that they have made a much better go at life than the VA newcomer. Why would they seek council from the person whom they believe to be the cause of their pain and misery? This can be a difficult hurdle for the VA newcomer to clear. They may need some acknowledgement for the courage it took to admit their powerlessness over violence, and the strength it takes to remain on the VA beam. This VA may be seeing where their side of the street ends and their partner's begins, realizing that they are not the only one in the relationship that may have a problem with violent behavior. Here it can be possible for both partners to blame each other and wonder when the relationship will ever be happy, or if it has ever been.

It may take every ounce of strength, recovery, and support the newcomer can muster to weather this storm. They will practice every tool at their disposal to behave kindly and with empathy. When they trigger, as all newcomers do, they will remove themselves as quickly as possible from the situation and seek to neutralize the trauma that leads them to trigger in these types of scenarios. Our VA will do whatever they must to disengage from old patterns, even though their partner may do everything in their power to pull the VA back onto the Drama Triangle. With perseverance and support from VAs and trusted professionals, our newcomer can become the loving and kind person their partner has longed for, and if the partner is also willing to look at their side of the street, this marriage can prosper and grow. Even if this marriage eventually comes to an end, this VA can navigate that transition in a healthy, loving and compassionate way. This has been my personal experience. After many years of VA recovery, I created a drama-free marriage, and years later, a divorce and cooperative co-parenting agreement where both parties, despite having differences and disagreements, experience being loved, respected and supported, one-day-at-a-time.

How about the single VAs who wish to have healthy romantic relationships? We have found it is best to have a solid foundation of recovery under our belts before attempting to date. Keeping our focus on recovery first and relationship second has proven to be the only way for us VAs to engage in healthy relationships. Many of us have tried to place relationships first and have found that both the relationship and our recovery have suffered as a result. Take the VA who finds that special someone, only to lose focus on recovery and slip back into "victim thinking." It may begin with prioritizing the relationship before VA meetings and step work, but eventually ends up in slipping back into old behavior and using power and control to meet their needs. Gripped by the delusion that they have been rescued by their new relationship and they can recover on their own, this VA sooner or later realizes the progressive nature of an addiction to violence. We cannot afford to judge this type of thinking, for we all need to hit our own rock bottom in our own time. We simply note, "There, but for the grace of God, go I."

For those of us who have had enough of the shame hangover, following the sage council of VAs with experience in recovery is paramount to steady and lasting peace of mind. How can we live a God-centered life if we put another person, place, or thing in front of our connection with our spiritual center? Before finding VA, we all put a desire to control others before healthy relationships. Now in VA, we understand how that behavior pulled us further from our dreams of healthy living. By continuing to practice these principles in all our affairs, we develop the skill to carry God's grace into any relationship.

Little will challenge one's recovery more than romantic relationships. We VAs have often experienced trauma regarding romance and meaningful connection with loved ones. These experiences have shaped our thinking and behavior regarding intimacy. Those of us who enter into intimate relationships, while in recovery, find ourselves confronted with many of our deepest fears and pains. For savvy VAs, this becomes an opportunity to examine our traumas and negative habits, in the interest of neutralizing and healing them. This allows us to move closer to those we care for, rather than pushing them away by acting out the shame of our past traumas. We have found that the deeper we commit to an intimate relationship, the deeper we must excavate those traumas. Here we root out the pain around having been victimized by people we trusted in the past. Many of our emotional injuries are those from childhood, when we were truly victims of something a child can have no control over. As an adult, in recovery, we do our utmost to refrain from seeing ourselves as a victim. Yet we must also recognize that, as children, we may have been victimized and were powerless to protect ourselves. A child needs to be protected, nurtured, given proper care and attention to grow into healthy adulthood. As children, most of us did not have these needs met. Instead, we were forced to fend for ourselves to survive. In a romantic relationship, all of these traumas can resurface to be healed. If we are vigilant with our recovery at this stage, we will find the support we need to neutralize these traumas and create loving, kind, and supportive relationships. It is important to note that the process of neutralizing trauma does not mean reliving these experiences and re-traumatizing ourselves. Many VAs have found solace in such trauma therapy as EMDR, EFT, TAT, and reframing. These processes, and others like them, allow us to heal and create new healthy anchors without "reliving" difficult experiences.

How about VAs who, for a multitude of reasons, are unable to have a family life? At first they may feel lonely and believe themselves to be Victims, whose plight can only be remedied by a good bout of self-inflicted depression. They see so much happiness around them and yet they find none for themselves. Can they find this connection in VA? The answer is "Yes." Many find nurturing connections by doing service in VA. Working with the still sick and suffering violence addict is a way to fill the void they may feel. These so-called loners often find they no longer feel alone, and in time, through the healing and repair of the 12 Steps, they drop the Victim act and find they can meet their need for love and connection in many healthy ways. These VAs may also find comfort in knowing they can devote themselves to many happy pursuits that those in families are denied.

Many who come to VA have issues with money. Whether we spend it too fast, hoard it, for fear of living with less, or lack the ability to make it, one thing is certain. Our relationship with abundance is as dysfunctional as our relationship with people. How many deals had we blown cutting someone out, playing the hurt victim and justifying a severed relationship? How many opportunities have we walked away from, blaming this person or that situation, when it was our own lack of mental discipline that put us on the Drama Triangle? How about those of us who amassed financial fortunes at the expense of others? How many of us compromised our own integrity and moral fiber for money and/or power? At the extreme, some of us have created great suffering for others, in pursuit of financial gain.

What about the contrary? Take the VA who remained small financially due to rescuing, perpetrating, or playing the victim. This VA gave up before the financial victory came. They somehow believed that life couldn't possibly include abundance for them. They stumbled through life looking for the next rescuer to pull them out of their rut and set them back on solid ground, only to slip right back again. This VA went through life alienating friends, family, and strangers, exhausting the resources of others and pouting because people wouldn't give them more, until they ended up in VA.

Now, the shame of past behavior coupled with facing the trauma underlying these unproductive habits can seem overwhelming. Lucky for these VAs, there are others who have endured the same pain of loneliness and have tread the path to recovery. These VAs are no longer alone. With time, we can all learn to meet our own need for financial security in healthy ways that add real value for ourselves and for society.

While working Step 12, we begin to understand that our financial abundance is directly related to the value we add to society, and our ability to contribute to society is directly linked to remaining free from drama. We learn to put down our habits of using coercion and manipulation to meet our needs for financial safety and security. Instead, we place our faith in God, by better utilizing VA's tools and focusing on how our actions serve others. In this way, our relationship with financial prosperity mirrors our relationships with people.

This commitment to practicing these principles in all our affairs is paramount in keeping a neutral state of mind during the turning of fortune's wheel. How often, even with experience in VA, do we allow Victim thinking to change a financial opportunity into financial struggle? How often do we allow our fear to get the better of us, trigger into seeing ourselves as Victims, and use guilt, coercion, or threats, to force another into becoming our savior or patsy? If we find our thinking has fallen from service to self-preservation, we can be confident that we have triggered and are now whirling around the Drama Triangle. This is a good recipe for either winning at someone else's expense or getting dropped from the deal. Hopefully by now, we have developed the ability to hold our tongues and remove ourselves before damaging our cause. This can be a wonderful opportunity for identifying the trauma that launched us into the trigger. Doing some work to neutralize our trauma before re-engaging in the endeavor is proof of our spiritual awakening and reliance on God. Each trigger is a doorway into our damaged thinking and gives us a starting point from which to change our pattern from reliving pain and fear to experiencing safety, security, and contribution toward a better life. By clearing the trauma, we change our thinking patterns and create better opportunities for true abundance. A state that brings value to all parties involved.

So how do we practice these principles in all our affairs regarding financial success? Here we keep a close eye on whether our desire for money overshadows our need to contribute to the wellbeing of others. We realize that meeting our need for safety and security while sacrificing our need for contribution is far from the ultimate victory. Our focus becomes increasing our wealth by improving the lives of others. We strive to utilize our God given gifts to enhance the world around us and to add to the wellbeing of those who share our little blue world. In Steps 4, 6, and 7 we began to understand that to gain wealth at the expense of others could be a violent act. In Step 12 we focus on the opportunities we have created by remaining free from drama. We use our time and energy to create wealth for ourselves and others, simultaneously. We no longer allow ourselves to play the rescuer. Instead, we strive to meet our first 5 basic needs while genuinely serving others. This service to others meets our sixth need, Contribution, and brings us even greater wealth. The gratitude we feel in recognizing how far we have come from our violent beginning fuels us further to help others and practice these VA principles in all our affairs. Here we begin to understand that by serving others we serve a higher purpose. In this way we began to redefine what we mean by wealth. Drawing back to the origin of the word, we understand that wealth has as much to do with our spiritual and psychological well being as our financial abundance.

As we found in our Fourth Step inventories, many of us were motivated by fear regarding money and abundance. Our chief worry was, "What if I can't find enough of it?" Now in Step Twelve we find that fear gradually leaves us. It is replaced with a confidence that God can and will guide us to better ways of creating wealth, financial or otherwise. The evidence is plain from our time in recovery. By this point most VAs can draw on experiences of having been delivered from fear and shame into faith. This faith has gradually become unshakable. The VA newcomer reminds us of what it was like in the early days of our recovery. The difference between then and now is nowhere short of a miracle for most of us. We have transformed from a fearful person into one who has found a spiritual connection and confidence. We now understand that life can be lived peacefully. Not only by the Gandhis of the world, but also by those of us who were once broken and lost.

In Step 12, we learn to give assurance to others simply by our example of living drama free. We no longer fear losing our wealth because we recognize that our troubles can be transformed into great value. Our material condition is no longer separate from our spiritual condition. The strength of our connection to God has led us to fewer triggers and less time on the Drama Triangle. This newfound neutral state has miraculously led us to better relationships, more financial abundance, increased gratitude and deeper spiritual calm; in other words, greater wealth. Wealth we are now able to share in all our affairs.

How about our thinking regarding personal importance, power, ambition, prestige, and leadership? Doesn't every healthy person strive to achieve his or her best? What child doesn't love the feeling of victory on the playground or the sense of accomplishment from completing a challenging task? We have already established that we all need Security and Variety, but when it comes to expressing our need for Significance in healthy ways we VAs are at a disadvantage. Regardless of our socioeconomic background, we have repeatedly used power and control to meet our need for Significance. Honestly understanding that we are special and important to others can be new to us. Equally foreign is the practice of asking our family, friends, and colleagues for simple expressions of our importance. Rather, our pasts are full of drama and failure to meet our need for Significance by healthy means. Take the woman who withholds sex from her partner as a punishment for a misunderstanding. She feels completely justified in her partner feeling as insignificant as she does. How about the man who withholds money for the same reason? This fellow might be in the habit of causing pain to another in order to believe he is significant. Both this woman and man put themselves in the "One-up" position, to believe themselves superior. However by using this strategy they fall short of the joy that comes with an authentic connection. Only by training oneself to remain off of the Drama Triangle and to ask for help in meeting one's needs does this pair begin to understand the pleasure of meeting their need for Significance while simultaneously meeting their need to Contribute to another's wellbeing.

How about the teenager who throws a tantrum, slamming doors or hiding away to gain what they think is power in their lives, or the child who whines as a means of calling attention to their need for Significance? We VAs have spent lifetimes developing ways to manipulate others into "showing us respect." The father who beats his children and wife; the mother who rescues by allowing herself to be a doormat then lashes out with judgment and shaming language; the children who rebel; the list goes on and on. How about the victim thinker stuck in believing that life owes them something? Perhaps, as a child, this VA was terrorized by adults many times their size or, just as damaging, was abandoned and given little or no attention. We can easily empathize with this child who believed that life owed them something better. This child, like all of us, shared the need for Safety, Security, Love, Connection, and to feel Significant. Now as an adult, this VA can no longer afford to live by the same patterning that trained them into thinking like a Victim.

Many of us were poor losers who whined and moaned, making excuses for our failures. When we stumbled we quit in a huff, became belligerent or wallowed in depression. Perhaps we played the braggart and covered our inadequacies by boasting about our superiority. Whether we wallowed in self-pity, hid out in fear or rushed in like a siege we all share the same defeat through Violence. Somewhere deep in our unconscious minds we clung to the idea that we were Victims. This thinking brought us to our knees and created pain and suffering for ourselves and those around us. Today, we must right size our desire for personal importance and power. When we work VA's 12 Steps we learn through self-empathy and reliance on God that these early traumas can be neutralized and we can meet our needs for Safety/Security, Variety, Significance, Love/Connection in healthy ways. Experience shows that once these 4 primary needs are consistently met, in a healthy manner, we can focus on our needs for Growth and Contribution. By practicing Step 12 we transform the poison of violence into medicine. By enduring the original traumas and neutralizing them through VA's 12 Steps and Tools we are free to pursue a life of Contribution and Growth. We become living examples of the power of violence recovery and begin to carry the message in our daily lives.

As savvy VAs, we have matured in our ability to abstain from the pull of the Drama Triangle and become people who no longer seek to dominate others in the pursuit of our needs. Instead, we work together with others to find mutually beneficial solutions. We no longer use shame, blame and guilt to bend others to our way of thinking. We understand that true leaders lead by peaceful example. Our success in cooperating with family, friends and community serves to inspire others. We become examples of people who have learned the value of a disciplined mind and begin to prefer the long-term gain of cooperation over the short-term gain of a violent fit. Though we strive to do our best and to serve others, we no longer depend on being distinguished among our peers in order to do God's work. Instead we recognize that a day lived with integrity, generosity and kindness is enough to feel fulfilled and profoundly happy. We refrain from seeking fame to be praised, and instead use our position to assist others. When singled out in our communities for good deeds done and notable achievements, we accept adoration with humility, knowing that the credit lies in our connection and service to God. We can be happy and fulfilled knowing we have helped another, just for today.

Still sweeter is the understanding that:

1. Through service to God we find esteem.

2. Satisfaction comes from commitments squarely met and difficulties overcome through service to God.

3. We can trust our intuition.

4. In God's eyes, we are each important.

5. We see evidence that love freely given meets our need for Growth and Contribution.

6. We are certain that we are no longer alone, isolated by our own thinking, spinning round and round on the Drama Triangle, living in our own self constructed prison.

7. We feel secure that we belong in God's plan and no longer are exiled to exist without Love and Connection.

These are enduring satisfactions of living that arise through the simple practice of serving our higher power. We have discovered that true ambition is the aspiration to live humbly under the grace of God.

This is the final chapter in our study of VA's 12 Steps; not an ending, simply a milestone in our continued and consistent recovery from addiction to violence. Most of us begin again at Step 1, since constant improvement is what we now seek in recovery. By now we clearly understand that by facing our problems we can overcome them. No longer are we content with sweeping our fears under the rug, hiding in corners or wrecking havoc. Instead, we live by the code of fearless perseverance and understand that we create our own good fortune by serving God and those we can help. We can now trust in our higher power to provide for us what we could not provide for ourselves: the joy of living. With each rotation of Earth, may we all continue to deepen our understanding of this simple prayer:

"God grant me serenity to accept the things I cannot change, courage to change the things I can, and wisdom to know the difference."

Slogans of VA

It's not "WHAT we do" it's the "WAY we do it."

Life happens THROUGH us not TO us.

From "fight or flight" to "I'm alright."

Easy does it.

One day at a time.

H.A.L.T.T.S. – Watch yourself when you get too Hungry,

Angry, Lonely, Tired, Triggered or Sick.

Keep your cool.

Pick your moment. Say it once. Let it go.

Mean what you say. Say what you mean. Don't say it mean.

Does it need to be said. Does it need to be said by me. Does it

need to be said by me now.

Hand on heart.

Hug yourself.

Make great memories.

Keep coming back. It works if you work it. So work it. You're worth it.

It's not for those who need it. It's not even for those who want it. It's for those who do it.

Don't leave before the miracle happens.

Stop, drop and trigger process.

Ask for help.

What am I feeling? What am I needing?

Slow it down. (SLOW. IT. DOWN. - Said slowly)

Anchor. Trigger. Craving. Compulsion. Consequences. (ATC)

Am I in fight, flight, freeze; blame, shame, guilt; persecutor, rescuer, victim?

Am I triggered?

Some catalysts for triggers are fear, threat, past trauma, limiting beliefs, shame or unmet needs.

Let the understanding, love and peace of the program grow in you one day at a time.

Author's note

This book and the program of Violence Anonymous are only possible because of the courage and inspiration of those brave founders of Alcoholics Anonymous. The author would like to acknowledge that this book was purposely patterned after the "Twelve Steps and Twelve Traditions of Alcoholics Anonymous," which was a thorough and complete explanation of the addiction of alcoholism and its program of recovery. Obviously a book on the 12 Steps of Violence Anonymous could not be written without drawing inspiration from such a great work.

Appendix A

Anger Management Courses - every city has one, most people there are court mandated and convinced that they don't have a problem, but I knew I had one and I got a lot out of it.

Domestic Violence Courses

Group Therapy

Men's and Women's Groups in your area

The Pathways to Peace Anger Management Workbook, by William Fleeman

Anger by William Gray DeFoore, Ph.D.

Compelled to Control, by J. Keith Miller

I Don't Want to Talk About It - Overcoming the secret legacy of male depression, by Terrence Real

The Mind Body Prescription – Healing the Body Healing the Pain, by John E Sarno, M.D.

Violent Partners – A breakthrough plan for ending the cycle of abuse, by Linda G Mills, J.D., Ph.D.

Insult to Injury - Rethinking our responses to Intimate Abuse by Linda G Mills, J.D., Ph.D.

The Five Love Languages by Gary Chapman

Anthony Robbins Personal Power II CD Program

Anthony Robbins Ultimate Relationship CD Program

The Three Faces of Victim – an overview of the Drama Triangle, by Lynne Forrest

A New Earth, by Eckhart Tolle

A Child Called It, by David Pelzer

The Body Keeps the Score, by Besser van der Kolk

Twelve Steps and Twelve Traditions – Alcoholics Anonymous

Alcoholics Anonymous "The Big Book" – Alcoholics Anonymous

Nonviolent Communication, by Marshal Rosenberg

Power vs Force, by David R Hawkins M.D.

Appendix B

The Step 1, 2, 3 Waltz meeting does the reading and writing listed here each week on Tuesday 7 PM and Wednesday 11 AM Central Time.

1. Start Step 1 – Intro to VA: Read "Step 1 - We admitted we were powerless…" on **page 13** to "Luckily for those who are willing to work it…" ; Write on "What Brought You to VA?"

2. Step 1 – Intro to the Drama Triangle & Victim Role: Read "Understanding The Drama Triangle" on **page 17** to "Exercise (2)": Write on the ways you see yourself as a victim

3. Step 1 – Rescuer Role: Read "Rescuer" on **page 23** to "Exercise (3)"; Write on the ways you see yourself as a rescuer

4. Step 1 – Persecutor Role: Read "Persecutor, Perpetrator Abuser" on **page 27** to "Exercise (4)"; Write down the ways you may persecute yourself and others

5. Step 1 - Read "Once I have humbled myself…" on **page 28** to "Exercise (5)" - More on the Drama Triangle: Write out 5 more ways you see yourself as a victim, rescuer or persecutor

6. Finish Step 1 – Read "My recollection of Step 1…" on **page 33** to "Exercise (6)": Write on "How are you powerless over violence and how is your life unmanageable as a result?"

7. Start Step 2 – Higher Power: Read "Step 2 - Came to believe…" on **page 39** to "Exercise (7)" (Agnostic Atheist Faithful); Write about "Your View of a Higher Power"

8. Step 2 – Putting Step 2 Into Action: Read "Putting Step 2 Into Action" on **page 47** to "Exercise (8)": Write on Feelings & Definitions "Exercise (9)"

9. Step 2 – Read "Niagara Falls Metaphor" on **page 49** to "Exercise (10)": Write a list of Anchors. Read "Tools for Stage 1 Anchors" - Change Attention, Change Location, Positive Anchors): Get up and do the positive anchor "Exercise (11)"

10. Step 2 – Read "Stage 2 Triggers" on **page 54** - stop at "Belly Breathing"; Write on Triggers & Effects "Exercise (12)" & Thoughts & Beliefs "Exercise (13)"; Read "Tools to use for Stage 2 Triggers" - Belly Breathing & Reframing (stop at Prayer)

11. Step 2 – Read "Tool for Stage 2 Triggers - Prayer" on **page 59;** Write a prayer "Exercise (14)"; Read "Tools for Stage 2 Triggers – EMDR & List of Techniques" (stop at Stage 3)

12. Step 2 – Read "Stage 3 Cravings" on **page 63** - stop at "Change Location"; Write on Cravings you experience "Exercise (15)"; Read "Tool for Stage 3 Cravings - Change Location" - stop at "Stage 4"

13. Step 2 – Over The Falls & Stage 4 Compulsions: Read "Stage 4"on **page 65** to "Exercise (16)"; Write on Compulsions & Strong Emotions "Exercise (17)" & Triggers "Exercise (18)"

14. Finish Step 2 – Stage 5 Consequences & Education: Read "Stage 5" on **page 72** to "Exercise (19)"; Write about consequences of your violent behavior

15. Start Step 3 – Letting go of Control: Read "Made a decision…" on **page 75** to "Exercise (20)"; Write on "In What Ways do I Need to Let Go of Control?"

16. Finish Step 3 – Tools: Read "Tools of Violence Anonymous" on **page 79** to "Exercise (21)"; Write on "In what ways do I need to let go of control?" "Exercise (22)"; Write on "How can I use the VA Tools to let go of control?"